Life BUILDERS
ADULT GROUP BIBLE STUDY

LEARNING TO PRAY LIKE JESUS

A 5-10 SESSION GROUP STUDY BASED ON THE LORD'S PRAYER

WES HAYSTEAD

Gospel Light

Gospel Light is an evangelical Christian publisher dedicated to serving the local church. We believe God's vision for Gospel Light is to provide church leaders with biblical, user-friendly materials that will help them evangelize, disciple and minister to children, youth and families.

We hope this Gospel Light resource will help you discover biblical truth for your own life and help you minister to adults. God bless you in your work.

For a free catalog from Gospel Light please contact your Christian supplier or call 1-800-4-GOSPEL.

PUBLISHING STAFF
Jean Daly, Editor
Pam Weston, Editorial Assistant
Kyle Duncan, Editorial Director
Bayard Taylor, M. Div., Editor, Theological and Biblical Issues
Mario Ricketts, Designer

ISBN 0-8307-1783-8
© 1995 Gospel Light Publications

How to Make Clean Copies from This Book

You may make copies of portions of this book with a clean conscience if:

- you (or someone in your organization) are the original purchaser;

- you are using the copies you make for a noncommercial purpose (such as teaching or promoting your ministry) within your church or organization;

- you follow the instructions provided in this book.

However, it is ILLEGAL for you to make copies if:

- you are using the material to promote, advertise or sell a product or service other than for ministry fund-raising;

- you are using the material in or on a product for sale;

- you or your organization are **not** the original purchaser of this book.

By following these guidelines you help us keep our products affordable.

Thank you,

Gospel Light

Contents

How to Use *Learning to Pray Like Jesus*

This exciting study of *Learning to Pray Like Jesus* has been designed to fit a variety of learning situations:

- You have a choice of course lengths (5 to 10 sessions).
- You have a choice of session plans (from 60 to 90 minutes).
- You have a choice of settings (classroom or home).
- You have a choice of meeting times (as part of Vacation Bible School, or Sunday mornings, Sunday evenings, weekdays or evenings) and frequency (once a week, every day or night, weekend retreat).

Whenever or wherever you can get a group of adults together to explore their interest in and concerns about prayer—this manual will be an invaluable guide.

This Leader's Guide

This leader's guide is a unique resource, offering a stimulating and enjoyable opportunity for group study or successfully teaching adults about God.

This leader's guide is unique because it—

- offers the flexibility of completing this study in from five to ten sessions;
- is based on the premise that a study of Jesus' teaching on prayer is a truly exciting adventure with great value for both long-term Christians and new believers;
- explores sound principles of a balanced, healthy prayer life encouraging people to expand their current prayer patterns;
- provides useful handles for helping people see the personal implications of the principles studied;
- includes proven strategies for enjoyable group interaction, enabling people to learn from the experiences and insights of others;
- requires very few additional supplies for class sessions. (An overhead projector is helpful, but not necessary. Blank paper, index cards, pencils, felt-tip pens are typical of the easily secured materials which help add variety and stimulate involvement. Suggested supplies are listed at the beginning of each session.);
- suggests practical actions participants can take to implement each session's learning.

Session Plan

Lessons are flexibly designed to be completed in one of three major time schedules:
- Option A—Sessions of 60-75 minutes each.
- Option B—Sessions of more than 75 minutes each.
- Option C—Two sessions each of about 60 minutes, extending the series from five to ten sessions..

Two important symbols are used in the session plans to aid in extending the lessons over two separate sessions.

1. This symbol indicates the **Two-meeting track** which allows you to extend lessons over two meetings each, giving group members more time for both discussion and prayer. The stop-and-go sign means to END your first meeting and BEGIN your second meeting at the point where the symbol appears in the session plan. Each of the lessons in this manual can thus be easily made into two complete sessions, for a total of ten sessions (Option C).

2. You will find instructions placed in boxes and marked with this clock symbol. This information provides optional learning experiences to extend a session over two meetings or to accommodate a session longer than 60-75 minutes (Options B or C).

Sample Session Plan

Getting Started

(10 minutes)

Each lesson begins with a choice of two relationship-building, experience-sharing activities which also help group members begin thinking of the main truth of the session.

Getting Started Option

This option will add 10 minutes to the Getting Started section, either reviewing highlights of the previous session or further introducing the current session.

Getting into the Word

(40 minutes)

Each lesson contains three to five major points, enabling class members to explore several issues and the implications for personal application. For example:

Step 1—First Point (15 minutes)

Complete instructions are given to enable the teacher to guide class members in helpful and enjoyable learning experiences.

Option

This option will add 5 minutes to the Step 1 section.

These optional activities explore aspects of each main point which could not be addressed in the shorter time schedules.

Note: If you are completing this session in one meeting, ignore this break and continue with the next Step.

Two-Meeting Track: If you want to spread a session over two meetings, **STOP** here and close in prayer. Inform group members of the content to be covered in your next meeting.

Start Option (10 minutes)

Begin your second meeting on a lesson by reviewing the main ideas from the first half of the session. (Suggested review activities are in each session.)

Getting Personal

(10 minutes)

Each session concludes with instruction and questions for summarizing session highlights, helping people make personal application of a main idea, with suggestions for implementing the ideas in practical ways.

Getting Personal Option

This option adds 5 minutes to Getting Personal, probing one personal issue studied.

A Few Teaching Tips

1. Keep It Simple. Teaching people about prayer can seem like an overwhelming task. The idea of actually talking with God is truly mind-boggling and intimidating. Avoid trying to reduce prayer to a matter of following formulas or mastering a variety of techniques. Participants will remember far more if you keep the focus on one issue at a time, seeking to keep your explanations as brief and simple as possible.

2. Keep It Light. Some of the session introductory activities in this manual are fun! This is intentional. Many people who most need this course are intimidated by the topic of teaching about God. Often there is fear that their own lack of knowledge will be exposed. People who are intimidated and fearful are not ready to learn. The light-hearted approaches are devices to help people relax so they can learn efficiently.

3. Keep It Significant. Because the course has some light touches does not mean its content can be handled frivolously. Keep clearly in mind—and repeatedly emphasize with your class—that this course is dealing with the awe-inspiring wonder of actually approaching the very presence of God. The insights gained in these sessions can make a big difference, not just in how people phrase their prayers, but in the overall vitality of their Christian lives.

4. Keep It Interactive. The learning activities in this manual provide a variety of involving experiences, recognizing the various learning styles which will be present in any group of adults. While some of the activities may not fit your preferred teaching style, by using this varied path to learning, you make sure that those who learn differently from the way you do will also have their needs met. A common type of involvement is having people share some of their experiences, helping one another expand understandings of various aspects of prayer and overcoming the barriers which interfere with prayer.

5. Keep It Prayerful. Both in your preparation and in each class session, pray earnestly that you and your class will be open to the truths about prayer which must be real to us if we are to enrich and deepen our communication with God.

To capture the interest of people in this course:

- Share some of your own experiences in prayer. To succeed in leading this course, you do not need to be an expert on theology, on prayer or on teaching methods. You do need to be honest about some of your struggles in seeking to understand and/or explain prayer.

- Point out that while societies and cultures change, and many life experiences are different for people today than for any preceding generation, God's desire for communication with His people has remained constant in all of human history. This course deals with principles which Jesus emphasized and which are at the core of effective prayer.

- Allow people to think and talk about their own prayer experiences. Many adults struggle with prayer, finding it difficult, an obligation that causes feelings of guilt for not achieving the level of prayer that they feel they are expected to maintain. This course is not a therapy workshop, but there is great value in allowing people to be open and honest in expressing their struggles. Admission of a problem is the first step in making progress toward growth.

Our Father in Heaven

Session Keys

Key Verse

"'Our Father in heaven, hallowed be your name, your kingdom come, your will be done on earth as it is in heaven.'" Matthew 6:9,10

Key Idea

God is honored when we pray recognizing His authority, wisdom and kindness.

Background

Among the many names used for God in the Old Testament, the prophet Isaiah was one of the few to address Him as Father:

"But you are our Father,... you, O Lord, are our Father" (Isaiah 63:16).

Isaiah also quotes God comparing His love with that of a mother:

"As a mother comforts her child, so will I comfort you" (Isaiah 66:13).

When Jesus taught His friends to address God as "Father," it was not a new idea, but it was definitely not how most people usually spoke to God. It is likely that at least a few eyebrows went up at Jesus' confident approach into God's presence. A certain uneasy twinge was probably felt by people used to thinking of God as stern, distant and unapproachable. Similarly, many people today have difficulty in viewing prayer as communication within a family.

It is not terribly difficult to envision God as King, Almighty Ruler of the Universe! Nor is it a great struggle to think of God as Holy, the Source of all that is just. Our minds can accept these lofty concepts.

However, it is another matter to advance into God's presence with the assurance of a beloved child, one who is cherished as only a loving father or mother can dote on a favored heir. We can nod assent to this concept, but to mix familiarity, boldness and reverence in our approach to God is much harder to do.

Our attitude and pattern of prayer grows out of our perception of the God to whom we pray. When we pray as Jesus taught us, we declare that through Jesus' sacrifice we belong to the holy and powerful Father who loves us. Addressing prayer to our Father in heaven is not a means to get God to do what we want done. Instead, it is the foundation of our declaration that we desire what He desires. The only way in which we can honestly state that we want His will to be done is if we recognize Him as the loving, all-knowing Father who has our best interests at heart.

Prayer is often misunderstood. It is sometimes viewed as a ritual performance that needs to be done in a certain manner or at specific times. Others view it as a vague, mystical activity that somehow impacts their relationship to a holy, awesome God. Or, it is seen as spiritual exercise or a contract in which the effort expended determines the benefits gained.

Jesus did not teach any of those attitudes towards prayer. Rather, both His example and His words taught that God our Father desires fellowship with His children. Jesus showed that our relationship with God, our heavenly Father, should be one of complete trust, love and obedience. We, as His children, should approach our Father in love and gratitude, not in fear and apprehension. Our prayer to God should be an expression of our confidence that He will hear us and will respond as a perfect parent who truly knows what is best, and who has both the power and the will to ensure what is ultimately good.

While the words of the prayer Jesus taught have been memorized and repeated by millions of believers for 2000 years, prayer is more than reciting the right words. Prayer is an expression of the heart inclined toward God.

As you prepare to teach this course, focus your thoughts on the importance of prayer in your own life and the lives of those you will teach. Set aside a definite time daily for personal fellowship with your heavenly Father, but not as an obligation. Practice the prayer experiences suggested in this session as opportunities for enjoyment, for basking in your Father's presence as one of His deeply beloved children.

Preparation

- Provide blank name tags and felt-tip pens. Make a tag for yourself.
- On a table at the front of the room, provide materials for one of these Getting Started choices:
  - Choice 1: Does God Really Care?—Duplicate copies of "Does God Really Care?" on page 21, providing one copy per person. Provide pens or pencils for those who need them.
  - Choice 2: Word Scramble—Make a transparency of "Word Scramble" on page 23. Set up the overhead projector, focusing it on a screen or a light-colored wall.
  - Make a copy of "When You Pray" on pages 25 and 27, and "Our Father" on page 29 for each participant.
- Provide Bibles for participants who may not have one. (It is preferable to provide identical Bibles so that any participants who are not familiar with locating passages can easily be assisted by being given the page numbers along with the Scripture references.)
- Provide a blank index card and a pen or pencil for each participant.

Session 1 at a Glance

SECTION	ONE-SESSION PLAN		TWO-SESSION PLAN	WHAT YOU'LL DO
Time Schedule	60 to 75 Minutes	More than 75 Minutes	60 Minutes (each session)	
Getting Started	10	10-20	20	Get Acquainted— Introduce Topic of Prayer
Getting into the Word	40	60-75	40	
Step 1 Jesus' Pattern of Prayer	10	20	20	Explore Bible Verses on Jesus' Times of Prayer
Step 2 Jesus' Instructions About Prayer	15	20	20	Identify Key Factors in Effective Prayer
			Session 2 Start Option: 10	
Step 3 What Jesus Taught About the God to Whom We Pray	15	20	20	Discuss the Meaning of the Opening Verse of the Lord's Prayer
(Step 4 Option) Prayer and God's Will	(10)	(10)	15	Discover How to Pray According to God's Will
Getting Personal	10	10-15	15	Plan a Specific Time to Pray

Session Plan

Leader's Choice

Two-Meeting Track: This session is designed to be completed in one 60- to 75-minute meeting. If you want to extend the session over two meetings and allow group members more time for discussion, **END** your first meeting and **BEGIN** your second meeting at the stop-and-go symbol in the session plan.

The boxes marked with the clock symbol provide optional learning experiences to extend this session over two meetings or to accommodate a session longer than 60-75 minutes.

Getting Started

(10 minutes)

Choice 1—Does God Really Care?

Welcome people as they arrive and suggest they make and wear name tags. Distribute copies of the "Does God Really Care?" worksheet. Encourage people to work in pairs or trios to mark each item, then compare their ratings with those of others. It is likely that most items will be marked fairly high.

After people have had time to mark the sheet and compare with others, ask for volunteers to share some items they marked as "Cares Deeply" and some that were marked "Cares a Little" or "Who Cares?" Then invite others to tell which item they indicated that they would be most likely to pray about, and which they would probably be least likely to mention in prayer. After several have shared, ask for a show of hands of those who said the item they would be most likely to pray about was also one they marked that God cares about. Similarly, was the item people said they would be least likely to pray about also ranked low as a concern of God's?

After people have shared their responses and thoughts, make this statement: **Obviously, some issues and experiences are more important and deserve more care than others. However, if someone really believes God cares about the details of life, while someone else believes most of those things are of little or no concern to God, which person would you expect to pray more often about daily living?** (A person who expects God to listen and respond to things he truly cares about would be more likely to pray about things he or she felt mattered to God. A person who feels God may not be interested in something would be likely to ask, "Why pray about it?")

Lead into this study by saying **We are beginning a study of prayer and what Jesus taught about it. A logical starting point would seem to be to determine whether or not God really does care about what goes on in our lives. If He doesn't, there's not much point in praying about our daily concerns.**

Lead a brief opening prayer, asking God's help in gaining insights into the value and practice of effective prayer.

Choice 2—Word Scramble

Welcome people as they arrive and suggest they make and wear name tags. Turn on the overhead projector and call attention to the scrambled words (p. 23) on the screen. Participants work in pairs or trios to unscramble the words and match them to the definitions on the page. As people work, be ready to greet new arrivals and involve them in this activity. (Answers are: petition, supplication, thanksgiving, communication, praise, confession, submission and adoration.)

Give a signal to gain everyone's attention. Welcome participants to this session. Then invite volunteers to tell the words which they unscrambled and the definition

of each term. Ask **From your experience, why is that an important aspect in prayer?** Summarize this activity by saying **There are many words which describe important aspects of prayer. In this session we're going to begin exploring prayer, considering both our own experiences with prayer and the example and teaching of Jesus about prayer.**

Lead a brief opening prayer, asking God's help in gaining insights into the value and practice of effective prayer.

Getting Started Option: Prayer Stories

This option will add 10 minutes to the Getting Started section and will help people continue to get to know each other while encouraging further thinking about prayer.

After completing one of the Getting Started activities, say **Before we focus on what Jesus taught about prayer, we're going to take a few minutes to share with each other some of the very real experiences, both positive and negative, that we have had with prayer.** Divide the class into groups of no more than four or five. Then instruct the group members to share with each other times when prayer has been difficult for them. To help people feel free to share honestly, briefly tell about a time when you struggled with prayer. Then comment: **If prayer were always easy and enjoyable, we'd all do a great deal more of it than we do.**

Allow groups up to five minutes to share; then invite participants to briefly tell of times when prayer was a positive, meaningful experience. Again, share an incident from your own experience to set the tone, keeping your example simple enough that people will not be intimidated into trying to "match" a powerful exploit.

Getting Into the Word
(40 minutes)

Step 1—Jesus' Pattern of Prayer (10 Minutes)

Introduce this segment by commenting In this series we'll be focusing on what Jesus taught His disciples about prayer. Before we explore what Jesus *said* about prayer, let's begin by considering several incidents which show what Jesus *did* about prayer. Divide the class into groups of no more than four or five. Assign each group one of the following passages to read and then discuss what those verses reveal about Jesus' pattern of prayer. (It is not necessary to assign all the passages, as they essentially reinforce the same fact, that Jesus regularly set aside time and place for prayer. If you have more than seven groups, assign the same passage to more than one group.)

- Matthew 14:22-25
- Mark 1:35-39
- Luke 3:21-22
- Luke 5:15-17
- Luke 6:12-16

- Luke 9:18-20
- Luke 9:28-32

Allow groups three or four minutes to read and talk about their assigned verses. Then ask for volunteers to share what they discovered about Jesus' example in prayer.

After several people have commented, sum up this section by asking a volunteer to read aloud Luke 11:1. Then comment **Jesus' closest friends had ample opportunity to observe the importance of prayer in Jesus' life. This request to learn to pray was not only motivated by reports of what John the Baptist's followers had been taught, but also by the repeated evidence of the powerful impact of Jesus' prayers.**

Option: Positive Examples of the Value of Prayer

This option will add 10 minutes to the Step 1 section.

Invite volunteers to tell about a person they have known whose prayers have been a positive example of the value of prayer. Share first about someone you have known, then allow participants to tell of their experiences.

If group members find it difficult to think of positive examples, invite them to consider the prayer example of the Apostle Paul. Invite volunteers to read aloud one or more of the following verses from Paul's letters:
- Romans 1:8-10
- Ephesians 1:15-18
- Philippians 1:4-6
- Colossians 1:9,10
- 2 Thessalonians 1:11,12
- Philemon 4

Then comment **It is obvious that the two great figures of the New Testament, Jesus and Paul, made prayer a significant part of their lives. Yet many of us who claim to belong to Christ, and who rely on the letters of Paul for much of our understanding about the faith, often struggle to pray as Jesus and Paul did. Would anyone, watching our lives and our patterns of prayer, be inclined to approach us and ask that we teach them to pray? This study is intended to help us identify and practice some of the powerful aspects of prayer, enabling us to truly pray as Jesus taught!**

Step 2—Jesus' Instructions About Prayer (15 Minutes)

Introduce this segment by commenting **Having considered the example of Jesus in making prayer a vital part of His life, let's explore some guidelines Jesus gave for effective prayer.** Distribute the "When You Pray" page. Instruct people to read the words of Jesus printed on the page, and for each passage, write one or two key words which describe an important characteristic of effective prayer. **For example, listen to this story Jesus told His disciples and think of a key word about prayer which the story illustrates.** Read Luke 18:1-8, then ask volunteers to suggest a key word (i.e., persistent, persevering). Write these words on the chalkboard or overhead under the heading "Keys To Effective Prayer." Ask **Why do you think Jesus said persistence in prayer was important?** Certainly not because God is in any way like the unjust judge

of the story who needed to be pestered to do what he did not want to do. Jesus clearly viewed prayer as evidence of faith (v. 8). Consistent prayer demonstrates and strengthens the faith of the one asking by focusing attention on God as the Provider of the answer.

Then allow about three minutes for people to read the passages and choose a key word for each one. (Likely key words include: Matthew 6:5-8: private, personal; Matthew 7:7-11: ask, seek; Matthew 21:22: believe; Mark 11:25: forgive; John 14:13,14: authority.)

Ask for volunteers to share the key word they selected for each passage. Add these to the chalkboard or overhead as they are mentioned. Then invite comments from people about why they think Jesus said each one was a key to effective prayer. Be prepared to clarify or expand on people's ideas:

- Matthew 6:5-8: private, personal (Prayer is an expression of the relationship between a person and God, not a vehicle to impress other people. When praying with others, great caution must be exercised to avoid the natural temptation to phrase our prayers to win the favor of people.)

- Matthew 7:7-11: ask, seek (God wants us to ask Him for our needs to demonstrate our recognition that He is truly the one in charge.)

- Matthew 21:22: believe (Obviously, there is no benefit in asking God for something without believing that He has both the power to provide and the loving wisdom to know what is best for us. Asking in prayer is not at all like rubbing a rabbit's foot or knocking on wood or entering a sweepstakes in the vague hope that "it can't hurt and it might help." Effective prayer is based on trust, not just that God hears, but that He cares and will do what is best.)

- Mark 11:25: forgive (Jesus never gave any instructions about the format of a prayer, or the physical posture of the one praying. He focused instead on our attitude, and not just our attitude towards God. Clearly, our relationship with God is powerfully interconnected to our relationship with other people.)

- John 14:13,14: authority (To pray "in Jesus' name" is far more than tacking a phrase on the end of a prayer. We have been given the privilege and authority to claim our relationship with Jesus as our entree into God's presence. By using this authority, that which we ask is qualified by a desire to be asking in accordance with what Jesus Himself desires. In other words, effective prayer is not merely representative of our personal desires, but a deep longing to be part of the work Jesus came to do.)

Option: Thinking and Praying

This option will add 5 minutes to the Step 2 section.

Let's take some time to think and pray, putting into practice at least one of the key ideas we have just considered. Encourage people to choose one of the key words they wrote on the "When You Pray" page. Then instruct them to spend a few moments thinking privately of the implications of praying so that the selected key word is given full consideration. **For example, if I had chosen the key word "persis-**

tent" as a factor to consider, how would my praying be influenced? After a few people respond, guide the group in a few minutes of silent prayer in which each person seeks to implement the key word chosen.

Note: If you are completing this session in one meeting, ignore this break and continue with Step 3.

Two-Track Meeting: If you want to spread this session over two meetings, STOP here and close in prayer. Encourage people to keep the "Keys to Effective Prayer" in mind in their own prayer times during the coming days. Inform group members that your next meeting will focus on the opening verse of the Lord's Prayer.

Start Option: Examples of Effective Prayer (10 Minutes)

Begin your second meeting by inviting group members to form pairs or trios and share with each other one way in which thinking about the "Keys to Effective Prayer" was helpful during the past week. Be prepared to share an example of your own to help people feel comfortable talking about their own prayer experiences. After several minutes of interaction, invite volunteers to share with the entire group one incident that was discussed in their smaller group. Then continue with Step 3 and conclude the session.

Step 3—What Jesus Taught About the God to Whom We Pray (15 minutes)

Introduce this segment by this comment: **Remember that when Jesus' disciples asked Him to teach them to pray, He responded by giving them a simple, yet profound example rather than a set of instructions. The prayer He gave them has proven powerfully useful over the centuries as both a means of directly addressing God, and as a model from which to learn about prayer. The most obvious thing we note as we consider this prayer is what it reveals to us about the God to whom we pray.**

Note: While most people in your group are likely to have a long-term familiarity with the wording of the Lord's Prayer from the *King James Version* of the Bible, this course uses the wording of the *New International Version* to help people gain something of a fresh perspective and to aid them in phrasing prayers as simply and directly as possible.

Divide the class into at least three groups with no more than four or five people in each group. Distribute the "Our Father" page to each individual and assign each group one of the three words featured on the page ("Father," "Hallowed," "Kingdom"). Each group is to look up and read the verses listed under their assigned word. If you have more than three groups, you may divide the Scriptures among the groups which have been assigned the same word.

After reading the assigned verses, the group members are to share with each other any insights the verses provide into the use of the assigned word within the Lord's Prayer. Allow four or five minutes for groups to read and talk.

Invite a volunteer from each group to read aloud one verse that group read and then share one insight gained. Be prepared to clarify or expand on comments from the groups:

Father—This name was not commonly used in referring to God prior to Jesus, but it was used occasionally. Several Old Testament references also mention God as mother (Isaiah 49:14, 15 and 66:13). The parent/child imagery of these references clearly conveys God's powerful love for His people growing out of a deep sense of belonging. There is recognition of the imperfection of human parents, but God as Father is clearly not tainted by that. (**Note:** The term "Father in heaven" reflects both God's transcendence of human limitations as well as respect for the Jewish reverence towards the name of God.) It is also clear that recognizing God as our loving Father in no way casts Him as indulgent or accommodating towards us. Far from separating the ideals of God as loving and God as holy and righteous, this term shows that it is precisely because of God's love for His children that He disciplines us when we fall short of His perfection. (See Hebrews 12:5-11.)

Hallowed—The phrase "hallowed be your name" is the first of six petitions in this prayer. Jesus is not merely stating that God is holy, but is asking that this crucial attribute of God's nature will be fully recognized on earth. We see the failure of Moses to follow God's instructions (Numbers 20) was at root a failure to recognize God's perfection. Thus, it is obvious that asking for God to be given the honor and regard due Him has significant implications for the actions and attitudes of those who claim to be His children.

Kingdom—The word kingdom is used fifty times in Matthew's Gospel, usually as "kingdom of heaven." While the term refers to the total rule and authority of God in heaven and on earth, its focus in this prayer is looking to the triumph of God's purposes in human affairs. The second petition of the prayer links the desire for God's kingdom (authority) to be fully consummated so that God's will should be achieved on earth as fully as in the other realms under His perfect control. Obviously, to ask for God's kingdom to be established in human lives is to express a desire to submit to God's purposes, not to pursue personal, selfish objectives.

When groups finish sharing, summarize the link between the three words just studied: **Only when we recognize God as our loving Father are we able to truly desire to honor His perfection and to long for His rule in all areas of our lives. Those who view God as a celestial spoilsport or a stern, unfeeling judge will shrink from His holiness and fear the establishment of His kingdom.**

Option: An Ideal Parent

This option will add 5 minutes to the Step 3 section.

Point out that many people's family histories lead them to view the term "father" very negatively. Some were abused by their fathers, some were abandoned, some were ignored. Invite everyone to think of a person, male or female, who embodies some of the positive qualities they would associate with an ideal father. This person does not need to approach perfection, but to have demonstrated attitudes and actions desirable for an ideal father. Describe a positive characteristic of someone from your own experience as an example to help people in recalling someone from their own lives.

After a few moments of thought, invite volunteers to share one of the positive qualities they recognize in the person they thought of. As people talk, list the qualities on the chalkboard or overhead.

Conclude this sharing time by leading a brief prayer of thanks: **Thank You, Father, that You love us far more than any of our earthly fathers or mothers. And thank You for the people You have sent into our lives who have shown us glimpses of Your love and care for us.**

Step 4 Option—Prayer and God's Will (10 Minutes)

Read aloud Matthew 6:10: "Your kingdom come, your will be done on earth as it is in heaven." Then make this comment: **The second request in the prayer Jesus taught is for God's kingdom authority to be enforced, for His will to be done in our lives and in our world. Asking for God's will to be done relates to asking in Jesus' name.**

Remind the group of Jesus' promise in John 14:13 that He will do "whatever you ask in my name." **Asking in Jesus' name is not the means by which we get God to do what we want, it is the means by which we can become part of the fulfillment of what He wants—the achievement of His will.**

Praying according to God's will means asking for those things which are in accord with God's stated purpose. He has not given us authority to ask for anything we desire until our desires are guided by Him.

The main question therefore is, "How do we pray according to God's will— how do we know what we should ask for?" A key insight is given in John 15:7: "If you remain in me and my words remain in you, ask whatever you wish, and it will be given you." (Also see Psalm 37:4). **By nurturing our fellowship with God and making the Scripture a continuing part of our lives, we are assured that our prayers will be answered because our desires will reflect God's will. By following the example of Jesus in asking that God's will should be done, we keep our hearts and minds open to the possibility of God giving a different and better answer than what we had requested.**

Have people return to the same groups of no more than four or five each. Assign each group one of the following Scriptures which clearly declare an aspect of God's will for human life. It is not necessary to assign all the Scriptures.

- Matthew 5:21-24
- Matthew 5:43-45
- Matthew 28:18-20
- Mark 12:28-31
- Luke 5:29-31
- Luke 9:23-25
- Luke 9:46-48
- John 13:34,35

Instruct the groups to read their assigned passage to find what it indicates that God wants to happen in our hearts and in our world. Then, the groups are to decide what implications that understanding has for praying for God's will to be done.

As time permits, invite volunteers to share something for which they can pray that the Bible clearly states is God's will. Conclude this sharing with this comment: **Learning to pray for the things we know are God's will is an effective way to allow God to help us begin to desire those things. To start praying regularly for an annoying neighbor or an aggravating co-worker or a rebellious child will have a powerful impact on our attitude toward that person. Prayer changes the person praying at least as much as it does the person being prayed for.**

Note: Praying for the salvation of someone who has not received Christ is clearly in accord with God's will (1 Timothy 2:1-4; 2 Peter 3:9). However, it is clear from many places in Scripture that not everyone will be saved (Psalm 37:20; Matthew 25:46; Luke 13:3). The assurance of Scripture is that God will certainly answer prayers on behalf of the unsaved, giving them opportunities to respond to His love. But the pages of the Bible are also filled with accounts of individuals and nations which rejected God's invitation and were judged. There is no indication in Scripture that God ever forces anyone to repent and turn to Him.

Getting Personal

(10 minutes)

Take a few minutes now to plan how you will put into practice something that we've discussed about prayer. Give each participant a blank index card. **This card is to be our personal prayer reminder for the next few days. We're going to write four things on the card.**

First, on one side, let's write down a time each day when we will pray. Share the time you are writing on your card and invite volunteers to tell the group what they have written. Encourage people who do not already have a definite prayer time each day to think of a time they can set aside to concentrate on talking with God.

Second, turn the card over, and at the top, write the phrase "Father in heaven." Then directly under that, write one positive "parental" attribute of God which helps you want to talk with Him. Share an attribute you have written down and why you find it helpful when you pray to think of God possessing that attribute. Invite volunteers to share the attribute they wrote down.

Third, in the middle of the card, write the word "hallowed," and directly below, write one way in which you can show honor and respect for God's perfect holiness. Share your intended action, then invite volunteers who haven't shared yet to do so.

Fourth, near the bottom of the card, write the word "kingdom." Just below that, write one thing you know is in accord with God's will that you can pray about in the coming days. Share your prayer request, then invite volunteers to share theirs.

Encourage people to place their reminder card wherever it will be most useful in reminding them about their prayer intentions: in wallet, purse, or book; taped to dashboard of car, refrigerator door, bathroom mirror, etc.

Getting Personal Option: Sharing Prayer Intentions

This option will add 5 minutes to the Getting Personal section.

Many times we may feel frustrated in not following through with our intentions to strengthen our prayer lives. One very helpful way to ensure following through on our plans is to enlist someone else as a prayer partner. Instruct participants to form pairs. If there is an uneven number of people in the group, be a partner with whoever needs one.

Instruct partners to each share with the other one or two items written on their index cards. Then the partners will pray for each other that they will follow through on their prayer plans for the coming days.

Before participants leave announce **The next session will focus on prayers for our daily needs: "Give us today our daily bread."**

Does God Really Care?

Mark the box that indicates how much you think God cares about each of the following:

	Cares Deeply	Cares a Lot	Cares Some	Cares a Little	Who Cares?
Personal problem with your employer					
You lost your keys					
You've been too busy to be neighborly					
Your finances					
Your TV viewing					
You've had a cold for two weeks					
Your political affiliation					
You can't find a parking space					
The color of the car you drive					
Your next vacation					

Circle the above items that you would be most likely to pray about.

Draw an ✗ beside the ones you would be least likely to pray about.

Why?

Word Scramble

Unscramble	Match With Definition
nipoteti	exchange of thoughts, messages, or information
plantiscoupi	expression of gratitude
knagstvignih	worshipful demonstration of love
mantoncimucio	statement or attitude of approval or admiration
saripe	solemn request to a superior authority
sincenoofs	admission of guilt
binsimosus	act of yielding to the authority of another.
roanotida	humble, earnest entreaty

Word Scramble

When You Pray

"'And when you pray,
do not be like the hypocrites,
for they love to pray standing in the synagogues
and on the street corners to be seen by men.
I tell you the truth,
they have received their reward in full.
But when you pray,
go into your room, close the door
and pray to your Father, who is unseen.
Then your Father,
who sees what is done in secret, will reward you.
And when you pray,
do not keep on babbling like pagans,
for they think they will be heard
because of their many words.
Do not be like them,
for your Father knows what you need before you ask him'" (Matthew 6:5-8).

Key Words:

"'Ask and it will be given to you;
seek and you will find;
knock and the door will be opened to you.
For everyone who asks receives; he who seeks finds;
and to him who knocks, the door will be opened.
Which of you, if his son asks for bread, will give him a stone?
Of if he asks for a fish, will give him a snake?
If you, then, though you are evil,
know how to give good gifts to your children,
how much more will your Father in heaven give good gifts
to those who ask him!'" (Matthew 7:7-11).

Key Words:

When You Pray (Continued)

"If you believe,
   you will receive whatever you ask for in prayer'" (Matthew 21:22).

Key Words:

"'And when you stand praying,
   if you hold anything against anyone, forgive him,
   so that your Father in heaven may forgive you your sins'" (Mark 11:25).

Key Words:

"'And I will do whatever you ask in my name,
   so that the Son may bring glory to the Father.
You may ask me for anything in my name, and I will do it'" (John 14:13,14).

Key Words:

Our Father

"'Our Father in heaven, hallowed be your name, your kingdom come, your will be done on earth as it is in heaven'" (Matthew 6:9,10).

The prayer Jesus taught His disciples is so familiar, we often fail to consider the powerful impact of the words when we say them. Look up these other Bible references to see what insights they give about three important words.

Our Father—the parent/child relationship of God and His people
- Isaiah 49:14,15
- Isaiah 63:16
- Isaiah 64:8
- Isaiah 66:13
- Hebrews 12:7-11

Insight gained:

....

....

Hallowed—to be valued or esteemed as sacred, holy
(English Bibles use a variety of words to translate the original Hebrew and Greek terms. The words in parentheses are those used in these verses by the *New International Version*. Other translations may use other terms.)
- Numbers 20:12 ("honor")
- Isaiah 8:13 ("regard")
- Isaiah 29:22,23 ("acknowledge")
- 1 Peter 3:15 ("set apart")

Insight gained:

....

....

Kingdom—the rule of God, including his authority and work in human lives
- Matthew 3:2
- Matthew 4:17
- Matthew 7:21
- Luke 17:20,21
- John 3:3-5

Insight gained:

....

....

Our Daily Bread

Session Keys

Key Verse

"'Give us today our daily bread.'" Matthew 6:11

Key Idea

God is honored when we recognize our dependence upon Him for the necessities of our lives.

Background

The small boy danced into the house, gleefully waving the trinket that his grandfather had bought him at the store. "Why did you buy him that junk?" the boy's parents glared at Grandpa. Grandpa shrugged his shoulders and grinned mischievously. "He told me he needed it," was his logical explanation.

Many people wish that prayer worked like that small boy's request to his grandfather. "Wouldn't it be great if I just told God I needed something, and He'd deliver right away?"

Would it be so great?

Even earthly parents—and grandparents—know that Grandpa's well-intentioned gifts can create a spoiled child. "I know I shouldn't be so easy," Grandpa admitted, "but it's so much fun to buy him stuff!" Grandpa knew all too well that his grandson didn't "need" that trinket, and he even knew that it wouldn't be long before his grandson would discard the trinket and start asking for something new.

Fortunately, God is not a kindly grandfather who indulges our every whim. Jesus teaches us to pray to the all-knowing, all-loving God who provides what we truly need, which often may turn out to be very different from what we are convinced we want.

When Jesus prayed, "Give us this day our daily bread," He taught us to ask for what we need "this day". It is tempting to look to the future, asking God to take care of situations that haven't occurred yet. It sounds so comforting to think of God going ahead of us, sweeping our path clear of obstacles. Instead, the repeated promises of Scripture show that He will be with us at the very moment we need Him. Prayer is not an insurance policy or savings account to assure a comfortable future. It is a living, daily communication that makes us aware of God's active presence in the immediate present.

One issue this session addresses may be the most difficult of all problems related to prayer: God's answers (or seeming non-answers) to our prayers. People often wrestle mightily with trying to understand why some prayers seem to get answered and others do not. This session will examine some of the basic principles regarding the requests we make of God. Often, we ignore biblical prerequisites for petitioning God because of our tendency to focus more on gaining our request than gaining God's purposes. However, even when we earnestly seek His will, a degree of mystery still challenges our faith. When seemingly all the guidelines of Scripture have been followed, but no answer is seen, questions and doubts gnaw at us. Often in such times we find it difficult to accept that God's answers are sometimes much different from what we ask for. As humans, our view of life is limited, contrasting with God's eternal perspective which knows much better than we do. Those limitations keep us at times from understanding what God is doing. Frequently, after the pain and pressure of the immediate situation has passed, we are able to look back and see God's remarkable answers. But sometimes, unable to see any evidence of God's presence, we must simply continue to trust that "in all things God works for the good of those who love him, who have been called according to his purpose" (Romans 8:28).

Preparation

- Provide blank name tags and felt-tip pens. Make a tag for yourself.
- On a table at the front of the room, provide materials for one of these Getting Started choices:
  - Choice 1: Asking for Help—Make a transparency of "Asking for Help" on page 41. Secure an overhead projector and focus it at the front of the room.
  - Choice 2: Boy, Do I Need...Boy, Would I Like...—Mount two large sheets of newsprint or butcher paper on opposite walls. Across the top of one, letter, "Boy, Do I Need..." and across the top of the other, letter, "Boy, Would I Like...." Provide several felt-tip pens by each sheet. Write or sketch on each sheet two or three responses you would make to complete that statement.
- Make a transparency of "The Privilege of Asking" on page 43.
- Option: Responding to the Privilege of Asking—Provide blank paper and two or three colored felt-tip pens for each group of four to six people. Have masking tape ready to use in displaying the completed samplers.
- On each of six poster board sheets, letter one or two of the words from Matthew 6:11: "Give," "us," "this day," "our," "daily," "bread." Mount the six posters so they are equally spaced around the walls of the room.
- Duplicate "Guidelines for Asking" and "My Requests" on pages 45 and 47, providing one copy of each page per person. Cut the "My Requests" pages in half. Provide pens or pencils for those who need them.
- Have Bibles ready for those who do not bring them.
- Option: Answers to Prayer—On a sheet of poster board or on the chalkboard, letter the first part of Ephesians 3:20, as follows:

  "Now to him who is able to do

  (3) _____

  (2) _____

  (1) _____ that we ask

  (4) _____ ,

  according to his power

  that is at work within us,"

  (Ephesians 3:20).

Session 2 at a Glance

SECTION	ONE-SESSION PLAN		TWO-SESSION PLAN	WHAT YOU'LL DO
Time Schedule	60 to 75 Minutes	More than 75 Minutes	60 Minutes (each session)	
Getting Started	10	10-20	20	Get Acquainted—Introduce Prayers of Petition
Getting into the Word	40	60-75	40	
Step 1 The Privilege of Asking	10	20	20	Explore Reasons to Ask God
Step 2 Meeting Our Needs	15	20	20	Analyze the Request for Daily Bread
			Session 2 Start Option: 10	
Step 3 Guidelines for Asking	15	20	20	Discover What to Ask for and How to Ask
(Step 4 Option) Answers to Prayer	(10)	(10)	15	Discuss Answers God Gives
Getting Personal	10	10-15	15	Write Specific Prayer Requests

Session Plan

Leader's Choice

Two-Meeting Track: This session is designed to be completed in one 60- to 75-minute meeting. If you want to extend the session over two meetings and allow group members more time for discussion, **END** your first meeting and **BEGIN** your second meeting at the stop-and-go symbol in the session plan.

The boxes marked with the clock symbol provide optional learning experiences to extend this session over two meetings or to accommodate a session longer than 60-75 minutes.

Getting Started

(10 minutes)

Choice 1—Asking for Help

Welcome people as they arrive and suggest they make and wear name tags. Call attention to the "Asking for Help" transparency and instruct people to find a partner and ask him or her to complete one of the statements about asking for help. Explain (humorously) that the "best" way to succeed in this activity is to be the first one to ask someone, "Which statement do you want to complete?" While the other person responds, the first person has a little extra time to think of what to say next. After both partners have completed a statement, they split up and find new partners and repeat the process. Each person is to try to converse briefly with the maximum number of people possible in the time allotted.

After five or six minutes, invite volunteers to share interesting ways they heard the statements being completed. Then comment: **This session will focus on the requests we make of God. Often our attitude towards asking other people for help will color our approach towards God. So, we will explore the kinds of requests God has told us He is always ready to hear, and will discover what God has promised to do in response to those requests.**

Choice 2—Boy, Do I Need...Boy, Would I Like...

Welcome people as they arrive and suggest they make and wear name tags. Direct people to the two large sheets of paper and ask them to write or sketch (on the appropriate sheet and using the felt-tip pens provided) one or two things they really *need* and one or two things they would really *like*. Encourage people to compare their responses with what others write.

After five minutes, invite volunteers to comment on their impressions of what people put on the two sheets. **Are there any obvious differences between the two sets of responses? Any similarities? What makes something a real need instead of just a desire? Are there valid needs other than for physical survival or health?**

After several people have responded, wrap up the discussion with a remark like this: **I trust these moments of thinking about needs and desires will prepare all of us to consider in this session the things we ask God to do for us.**

Getting Started Option: Petition, Supplication, Invocation

This option will add 10 minutes to the Getting Started section.

After completing one of the Getting Started activities, say **Before we look at the next section of the Lord's Prayer, let's look at what Jesus and Paul said about approaching God with our requests.** Divide into at least four groups of no more than five or six in each group. If the class is large, have more than one group do the same

assignment. Assign each group one set of verses to read to find clues about Jesus' and Paul's attitude about asking God:

1. John 14:11-14
2. John 15:7,14-16
3. John 16:23-27
4. Ephesians 6:18-20; Philippians 4:6; 1 Timothy 2:1-4

After several minutes, ask volunteers from the first three groups to share what they discovered about Jesus' attitude toward asking. (Note: Seven times in John 14-16, Jesus encourages us to ask.)

Next, ask for comments on Paul's view of asking. Be sure the point is made that both Jesus and Paul shared a very positive view of asking God. In each case, the content and purpose of the requests is of great importance.

Before moving into the rest of this study, point out that there are two types of supplication or petition:

- **Personal Petition—making a personal request of God**
- **Intercession—asking on behalf of others.**

Getting into the Word
(40 minutes)

Step 1—The Privilege of Asking (10 Minutes)

Introduce this segment by noting: **We tend to think of asking only as a means of getting what we are asking for. Scripture clearly shows us additional reasons to petition God.**

With people in four (or more) groups of up to five or six in each group, assign each group one of the Scripture references listed on "The Privilege of Asking" transparency. **Read your verses, then talk in your group about how to complete the printed statement concerning our asking God for His help.** Allow two or three minutes, then call for volunteers to share their group's statement. While the wording may vary, the following points should be clearly stated. Add each point to the transparency as it is presented.

- Matthew 7:7,8—Ask God because God will answer, and because Jesus encourages us to do so.
- Matthew 7:9-11—Asking is a privilege of our relationship as children who come to a loving father.
- John 15:4,5—Asking links us to God's source of power (like branches drawing life from the vine). Asking is one of the ways we remain in Christ.
- John 15:7,8—Asking glorifies God. It demonstrates our dependence on Him, reveals His character, and prepares us so that He can work His purposes in our lives.

After these points have been made, ask **If a person never asks God for help, what does that indicate about his or her relationship with God?** (Obviously, the relationship is not close. To not ask for help implies either an ignorance of God's desires, a mistrust of God's intentions, a lack of belief in His power, and probably, a sense of self-sufficiency which does not recognize God's involvement in personal affairs.)

Option: Responding to the Privilege of Asking

This option will add 10 minutes to the Step 1 section.

Remaining in the same small groups as before, give each group paper and one or two felt-tip pens. Instruct each group to design a sampler (a piece of cloth embroidered with a design and a motto) which expresses an appropriate response to the privilege of being able to ask God about our needs. Suggest that the words and designs on the samplers be made to look as much like stitchery as possible. Be prepared to suggest one or two sample mottos to aid the groups in thinking of their responses: "It's great to know He wants me to ask," or "God: A Father who welcomes my requests."

As groups finish their sampler, mount them on the walls around the room. If time permits, read aloud the mottos "embroidered" on the samplers.

Step 2—Meeting Our Needs (15 Minutes)

Introduce this segment by reading aloud Matthew 6:11: **"Give us this day our daily bread."** Explain that the group is going to spend the next few minutes analyzing what this simple sentence conveys about what we can ask God to do for us. Call attention to the six posters which you have previously prepared with the words of Matthew 6:11 and then placed on the walls around the room. Instruct people to choose one poster.

When everyone has chosen a poster, have them form groups corresponding to their choices. Give these instructions: **You're going to have a stand-up discussion about the significance of the word, or words, on your poster. Consider these questions in your discussion:**

- What does that word say to you about making requests of God?
- If Jesus had used a different word in His prayer, how might our understanding of petitioning God be different from what it is?
- How significant is that word to the total meaning of the request?

Allow four or five minutes for people to talk. Move to the "Give" poster, and invite volunteers to share insights into making requests of God. After several people respond, add a clarifying comment, if needed, then move similarly to each of the next posters, in order. Ideas that should be emphasized include:

- **Give**—We are asking for gifts from God's generosity, not for payments we have earned.
- **us**—While prayer is often a very private experience, it is also a corporate one, a means of being connected to the needs and concerns of one another.

- this day—Jesus focuses our attention and concern on the present moment, not on the vague uncertainties of the future, nor looking back on that which is already past.
- our—Again, we are taught to look beyond our own personal concerns, addressing God as people who belong to a body of people.
- daily—Here we see the recurring nature of our needs and of God's provision. Yesterday's victories and blessings must be renewed on a continuing basis, otherwise they become stale.
- bread—Grains are a staple of our lives, not a luxury. We are taught to look to God for that which we need, not expecting Him to fulfill our whims and desires.

Option: The Benefits of Balance

This option will add 5 minutes to the Step 2 section.

Invite participants to consider the wisdom of a prayer recorded in the book of Proverbs. Read aloud the prayer found in Proverbs 30:7-9. Then, ask **What does this prayer add to our understanding of Jesus' request to be given daily bread?** Group members should identify the value of seeking to avoid the extremes of indulgence or poverty. A good test of the things we ask from God is to consider if granting the request will help us continue to seek His help and guidance.

Note: If you are completing this session in one meeting, ignore this break and continue with Step 3.

Two-Meeting Track: If you want to spread this session over two meetings, STOP here and close in prayer. Encourage participants to set aside time each day to ask God for specific daily needs. Inform group members that your next meeting will focus on guidelines for asking God.

Start Option: Sharing Prayer Requests (10 Minutes)

Begin your second meeting by inviting group members to form pairs or trios and share with each other one need for which they have been asking God's help. After each person has shared, group members pray for one another's requests. Then continue with Step 3, and conclude the session.

Step 3—Guidelines for Asking (15 Minutes)

To help people think about what they ask of God and the way in which they ask, distribute the "Guidelines for Asking" page, plus pens or pencils and Bibles to those who need them. Point out the first item under "What to Ask For," and explain that the two verses under each of the four items give clues to four important guidelines in what we can ask God for with assurance. Instruct people to fill in the blanks on the page as the group works together to discover the four guidelines. **Notice the first**

Scripture reference, Matthew 6:10 is the second verse of the Lord's prayer. Of course, you all know the word that fits in that blank line (your or thy). So the first clue to the first guideline is a prayer that God's purpose will be accomplished.

Point out that the second reference (Mark 9:24) is a statement by the anguished father of a boy possessed by an evil spirit. In one dramatic declaration, he expressed a remarkably familiar tension between competing forces. On the one hand, he declares, "I do *believe*." Then, as if recognizing the magnitude of what he is asking, he pleads, "Help me overcome my *unbelief!*"

State the first guidelines for which those two references are clues: **All our requests of God must be based on confident trust in God, a dependence that He truly knows and will do what is best in all situations. However, such trust does not always come easily for us, so faith is the first thing to ask of God, as that father asked of Jesus.**

Having used the first guideline as an example, lead the group through the other three guidelines, having them look up the references and then suggest what those verses indicate about what we are to ask of God. While people suggest various wordings for these guidelines, they should have little or no trouble getting the basic idea that we are to ask for:

2. A Personal Relationship with God

3. Development of Godly Character Qualities

4. Help with Daily Needs

After completing the "What to Ask For" section, move to the four points under "How to Ask." Invite volunteers to tell why each of the points is important in presenting petitions to God. Be ready to clarify comments on each point if necessary:

1. Believe because "without faith it is impossible to please God."(Hebrews 11:6). For example, in Jesus' own hometown, "he did not do many miracles there because of their lack of faith" (Matthew 13:58). **Note:** Faith is not just wishful thinking turned up a notch or two. It is very clear in Scripture that the issue is not *how much* faith or *how strong* our faith (see Matthew 17:20), but rather *in whom* we have placed our faith (Mark 11:22).

2. Be honest because the Lord already knows our hearts. When we recognize we are addressing the God who knows all about us, we become able to see through the facades we have erected. Thus we need to pray openly, expressing our true thoughts, feelings and motives.

3. Be specific because vague petitions bring no glory to God for there is no way to know if, when or how He answers.

4. Be persistent, not because God begrudges helping us and needs to be cajoled into answering, but as an expression of continuing faith and trust.

Option: To Know God Better

This option will add 5 minutes to the Step 3 section.

Distribute blank paper and pencils, then ask everyone to write out a simple prayer asking for a deeper, more personal relationship with God. **Write your honest thoughts and feelings about getting to know God better.** Assure people that this prayer will not be shared, but is to aid them in thinking clearly about their relationship and communication with God.

Step 4 Option—Answers to Prayer (10 Minutes)

Explain that you are now going to examine five answers God may give to our petitions. Lead the class in looking at each reference under these headings to discover the various answers God may give us. Encourage participants to share their thoughts on each answer discovered.

1. "Yes!"—Psalm 37:4; Proverbs 10:24

Ask **What do these verses tell us is one answer God gives to our requests?**

Be prepared to share from your own experience times when you received a "Yes!" answer to prayer.

2. "Yes, plus more!"—Ephesians 3:20

Point to the poster you prepared and note the blank lines. Invite people to look up Ephesians 3:20 and call out the missing words as you proceed: **Paul writes that God is able to do, not just *what* we ask, nor even (1) *all* that we ask, nor just (2) *more* than all that we ask, nor even just (3) *immeasurably* more than all that we ask, but immeasurably more than all we ask (4) *or imagine*! Our expectations are often more limited than what God intends to do for us or through us.**

3. "Yes, but wait."—Psalm 27:14; 2 Peter 3:8

Our timing is often very different from God's timing.

4. "No."—2 Corinthians 12:7-10

Paul, the same writer who penned Ephesians 3:20, received a clear "no" from God even though Paul repeatedly asked to have a severe affliction removed. God's answer was "no" because God knew Paul needed this testing in order to understand how God's power works through human weakness.

5. "No, I will do something better."—Jonah 4:1-4

Jonah was angry that God had spared Nineveh. Jonah did not want to accept the fact that God's mercy towards Nineveh was better than Jonah's desire for vengeance. Jonah is a classic example of how we tend to continue arguing our viewpoint against God, often after we have been clearly shown God's intentions.

As time permits, invite group members to share experiences when they received one of these answers to prayer.

Getting Personal
(10 minutes)

Distribute the "My Requests" page and invite everyone to write at least two requests under each of the three categories. **Keep in mind the guidelines we have explored about what we ask God to do.**

After several minutes, invite participants to find a partner, then share one or two of the requests each has written. Partners then join in prayer for those requests.

Getting Personal Option: Three Training Tips

This option will add 5 minutes to the Getting Personal section.

Conclude this session by sharing these "exhortations" about developing an effective prayer life:

1. You learn to pray by praying, not by discussing it in class, or reading about it. Like any other discipline in life, prayer will never get any easier until you start doing it consistently.

2. Pray for help with praying. If you find praying difficult, talk with God about the difficulties. Be honest and specific in describing where you struggle, but not just to register your complaints or present excuses. Present each one and ask God's help in dealing with it. Remember, it's just like talking to someone we love, and we all know how to do that.

3. Learn from others, but be yourself. Just because someone else gets up at 5:00 A.M. and spends an hour in prayer and meditation does not mean you have to adopt the same pattern. If regular prayer is a new experience for you, be willing to experiment and make adjustments. Start with a schedule you know you can follow, then expand it as you feel yourself growing.

Before participants leave, announce **The next session will focus on prayers of confession, asking God's forgiveness for the things we have done wrong.**

Asking for Help

The last time I asked someone for help...

Asking a relative or close friend for help makes me feel...

Asking a neighbor or casual acquaintance for help makes me feel...

Asking someone at work for help makes me feel...

The hardest thing about asking for help is...

The best thing about asking for help is...

The Privilege of Asking

"When you pray, do not keep on babbling like pagans, for they think
they will be heard because of their many words.
Do not be like them, for your Father knows what you need
before you ask him" (Matthew 6:7,8).

Question: If God already knows what we need, why bother to ask?
Answer: Read these passages to discover reasons we should ask God when we
have a need.

Matthew 7:7,8—Ask God because...

Matthew 7:9-11—Asking...

John 15:4,5—Asking...

John 15:7,8—Asking...

Guidelines for Asking

What to Ask for:

1. _____

"_____will be done" Matthew 6:10

"I do _____ ; help me overcome my _____ !" Mark 9:24

2. _____

"I want to know _____ ." Philippians 3:10

"My soul thirsts for _____ ." Psalm 42:2

3. _____

"...so that you may have great _____ and _____,.... Colossians 1:11

"If any of you lacks _____ , he should ask God." James 1:5

4. _____

"... in _____ , by prayer and petition, with thanksgiving, present your

_____ to God. Philippians 4:6

"Cast all your _____ on him because he cares for you." 1 Peter 5:7

How to Ask:

1. Believe.

2. Be Honest.

3. Be Specific.

4. Be Persistent.

My Requests

Personal Requests

Date	Request		Date	Answer

Requests for Family Members

Date	Request		Date	Answer

Requests for Others

Date	Request		Date	Answer

Thanks

Forgive Us Our Debts

Session Keys

Key Verse

"'Forgive us our debts, as we also have forgiven our debtors.'" Matthew 6:12

Key Idea

God is pleased when we admit the wrongs we have done and ask His forgiveness.

Background

"Don't loan money to a relative or friend," the businessman advised. "If you do, consider it a gift, not a loan, 'cause you'll either lose the friendship or the money." Frequent letters to advice columnists about unpaid debts among friends and family members indicate that this businessman knew whereof he spoke. Debts put a strain on any relationship.

In light of this observation, consider Matthew's version of Jesus' model prayer. Asking for God's forgiveness is phrased in monetary terms. While Luke quotes Jesus as praying, "Forgive us our sins" (Luke 11:4), Matthew's account reads, "Forgive us our debts" (Matthew 6:12). Perhaps Matthew's life as a tax collector made him especially sensitive to the problems of unpaid debts. No doubt he had seen debtors go to great extremes to avoid the tax man. When finally able to dodge no more, the pain of their fear and discomfort must have been evident.

If God were a celestial version of a tax collector, squeezing out the last drop owed, who would ever dare approach Him? Since everyone has offended God as well as others, prayer would be something to avoid at all costs.

But Jesus did not teach us to approach God as Judge, the One who sentences offenders. We pray to the loving Father, who made marvelous and costly provision to clear our debts completely, having nailed them all to the cross (see Colossians 2:13-15).

To make sure we do not take forgiveness lightly, we are told that the forgiveness we receive depends on the forgiveness we offer to any who owe us. The harsh tone of Jesus' story of the unforgiving servant (Matthew 18:21-35) illustrates the serious damage we do to ourselves and to others when we do not forgive. When we stack up all the real and imagined wrongs that others have committed against us, including those that have hurt us deeply and that we are unable to forget, their sum comes to no more than the few dollars ("a hundred denarii") Jesus said was owed to one servant by another. Then we look at the stack of our own lifetime of sins against God, both overt actions and well-hidden attitudes, and realize they are comparable to the millions of dollars ("ten thousand talents") owed by the first servant to the king. We realize how easy it is for us to overlook or excuse our own failings, while holding a grudge against another and how much our sins cost Jesus Christ on the cross.

It is not uncommon for people who have been deeply offended by someone to find it difficult, if not impossible, to forgive. Deep within us is a desire to even the score, to be sure the other person does not "get off the hook." Only when we look at these situations from God's perspective, and consider all that God has forgiven us, are we able to begin the difficult, but essential journey of forgiveness.

Remember, God's forgiveness is not intended just to absolve us, but to change us, to make us more like God Himself, people marked by His love and forgiveness; people able to bring reconciliation and healing into the stresses and conflicts of human affairs.

Preparation

- Provide blank name tags and felt-tip pens. Make a tag for yourself.
- On a table at the front of the room, provide materials for one of these Getting Started choices:
  - Choice 1: Confession Leads To...?—On a blank transparency or on the chalkboard, letter these statement starters:
    1. When I admit guilt to someone else, I usually feel...
    2. Admitting guilt is hard because...
    3. In human society, confession usually leads to...
    4. With God, confession leads to...
    Cover the last three statements with a sheet of paper.
  - Choice 2: Confused About Forgiveness?—Duplicate copies of "Confused About Forgiveness?" on page 61, providing one copy per person. Provide pens or pencils for those who need them.
  - Option: God's Promise to Forgive—A Bible for every four or five participants.
- Make a copy of "The Unmerciful Servant Melodrama" on pages 63 and 65 for each person.
- Provide blank writing paper and pencils for each participant.
- Provide Bibles for those who do not bring their own.

Session 3 at a Glance

SECTION	ONE-SESSION PLAN		TWO-SESSION PLAN	WHAT YOU'LL DO
Time Schedule	60 to 75 Minutes	More than 75 Minutes	60 Minutes (each session)	
Getting Started	10	10-20	20	Get Acquainted—Introduce Confession and Forgiveness
Getting into the Word	40	60-75	40	
Step 1 Confession: A Necessity of Life	10	20	20	Explore Reasons Confession Is Essential for Forgiveness
Step 2 Not Perfect; Just Forgiven	15	20	20 *Session 2 Start Option:* 10	Discuss Implications of Bible Passages on Forgiveness
Step 3 Steps to Forgiving Others	15	20	20	Analyze Jesus' Story of the Unforgiving Servant
(*Step 4 option*) Seeking Forgiveness From Others	(10)	(10)	15	Consider Steps to Take in Asking Another Person to Forgive a Wrong
Getting Personal	10	10-15	15	Personalize Psalm 51

Session Plan

Leader's Choice

Two-Meeting Track: This session is designed to be completed in one 60- to 75-minute meeting. If you want to extend the session over two meetings and allow group members more time for discussion, **END** your first meeting and **BEGIN** your second meeting at the stop-and-go symbol in the session plan.

The boxes marked with the clock symbol provide optional learning experiences to extend this session over two meetings or to accommodate a session longer than 60-75 minutes.

Getting Started

(10 minutes)

Choice 1—Confession Leads To...?

Welcome people as they arrive and suggest they make and wear name tags. Call their attention to the statement you wrote on a transparency or on the chalkboard: "When I admit guilt to someone else, I usually feel...." Give this instruction: **In the next few minutes, move around the room and find out how three other people in our group would complete that statement.** As others arrive, encourage them to mingle among the participants and ask people how they usually feel when admitting guilt to someone.

After several minutes, ask people to be seated, then ask for volunteers to share some of the feelings they heard mentioned about admitting guilt. Next, uncover the second statement "Admitting guilt is hard because..." and invite participants to suggest ways to complete this sentence. When someone suggests the idea that fear of punishment tends to make people reluctant to admit guilt, uncover the third statement "In human society, confession usually leads to...." Provide the completion to this statement yourself: **Confession usually leads to punishment. If you admit to breaking a law, the law demands justice.**

Conclude this Getting Started activity by uncovering the fourth statement "With God, confession leads to...." Ask the class to complete the statement. When the word "forgiveness" is offered, introduce the topic for this session: **Jesus taught us to pray for forgiveness. Such a request necessitates awareness of a need for forgiveness, an admission of having offended. In this session, we will explore the vital link between our prayers of confession and God's merciful forgiveness.**

Choice 2—Confused About Forgiveness?

Welcome people as they arrive and suggest they make and wear name tags. Distribute copies of the "Confused About Forgiveness?" page, providing pencils or pens to those who need them. Encourage people to work in pairs or trios to connect the parts of the six Old Testament prayers of forgiveness. If necessary, people may want to look up the verses in the Bible.

Once the verses are correctly completed, instruct people to talk with their partners about the question at the bottom of the page: "What impressions about forgiveness do you gain from these prayers?"

After several minutes of interaction, ask for six volunteers to each read aloud one of the prayers. Then invite responses to the question. Once several people have commented, introduce the topic for this session: **Jesus taught us to pray for forgiveness. Such a request necessitates awareness of a need for forgiveness, an admission of having offended other people and, most importantly, God Himself.**

In this session, we will explore the vital link between our prayers of confession and God's merciful forgiveness.

Getting Started Option: God's Promise to Forgive

This option will add 10 minutes to the Getting Started section.

After completing one of the Getting Started activities, say **Many people are reluctant to ask God for forgiveness, either out of a feeling they don't deserve it, or from a sense that a just and righteous God simply cannot or will not forgive what they have done. God is able to forgive our sins. God's love for His children is the begining point of His forgieness. I want us all to approach this study of confession and forgiveness by hearing some of the many promises of forgiveness God has already made to us.**

Assign one of each of the following references to seven people to look up and read aloud for the rest of the group to hear:

- Chronicles 7:14
- Psalm 86:5
- Jeremiah 50:20
- Matthew 26:27,28
- Acts 10:43
- Hebrews 8:12
- 1 John 1:9

After the verses are read, ask **What are the only requirements mentioned in any of these verses in order to receive God's promised forgiveness?** (humble selves, pray, seek God, turn from wickedness, confess sin). **In light of God's promises, how certain can we be of God's forgiveness?**

Read aloud one more Scripture: "Blessed are they whose transgressions are forgiven, whose sins are covered. Blessed is the man whose sin the Lord will never count against him" (Romans 4:7,8).

Getting into the Word

(40 minutes)

Step 1—Confession: A Necessity of Life (10 Minutes)

Introduce this topic by assigning two group members to read aloud Matthew 6:12, "Forgive us our debts, as we also have forgiven our debtors." and 1 John 1:9, "If we confess our sins, he is faithful and just and will forgive us our sins and purify us from all unrighteousness." Then ask **Why are forgiving others and confessing our own sins necessities for forgiveness?** Allow time for people to think and respond. The following points should be made.

- Forgiving others is evidence of an honest recognition of our own weakness and failings, which is a central ingredient in true confession. The person who refuses to forgive another builds a wall of resistance which makes that person unable to gratefully receive God's forgiveness.

Note: Point out that the process of forgiving others will be explored later in this session. First, attention will be given to our prayers of confession.

- In one sense forgiving others is like a transaction in which one party has to come across with confession before the other party comes through with the desired forgiveness. Leviticus 26:40-42 talks about the need for Israel to "pay for their sin." This concept is also reflected in the requirement to make restitution to anyone who has been wronged (see Numbers 5:5-7). Similarly, forgiving others is the required response of the person who has been forgiven.

- Confession is also a symbolic, ceremonial act, enabling the one confessing to envision his or her sins being removed as they are mentioned. Leviticus 16:20-22 describes the priest's confession with his hands on the head of a goat which is then released into the desert, symbolically carrying away the nation's sins.

- Confession is the necessary act of dealing openly and honestly with our sin so that change can take place. Failure to recognize or admit that we have done wrong keeps our sin from being exposed so that it can be cleansed. Proverbs 28:13 links confessing sin with renouncing it. Until it has been admitted, it cannot be turned away from. See Psalm 32:1-5 for a vivid description of the hopeless condition of someone who would not face up to sin, and the transformation which ensued once that sin was confessed.

- Confession is essential to allow cleansing from sin so that fellowship with God can be restored. In any relationship which has been marred by one party offending the other, reconciliation cannot occur until that offense has been dealt with. As the Psalmist wrote, "If I had cherished sin in my heart, the Lord would not have listened" (Psalm 66:18).

Note: Point out that confession is not a generic admission of vague or nebulous infractions. Confession is the admission of specific sins which have been recognized as offenses. As a Christian seeks to draw closer to God, the Holy Spirit and the Scriptures will make it clear what issues need to be dealt with.

Option: Three Parts to Confession

This option will add 10 minutes to the Step 1 section.

To go a little deeper into an understanding of what confession really involves, present the following points, asking volunteers to read aloud the verses which illustrate each one. Confession is much more than just saying "I'm sorry," which is often a quick response when a sin has been discovered. An apology is often simply a request to be excused from the unpleasant consequences of an action or attitude that will probably be repeated. There are three distinct aspects to a true, full confession.

1. Agree with God's judgment that specific attitudes and actions really are sins, grievous offenses against God's love and holiness.

"For I know my transgressions, and my sin is always before me. Against you, you only, have I sinned and done what is evil in your sight" (Psalm 51:3,4).

2. Ask God for forgiveness on the basis of Christ's death in which He paid the penalty for our sin.

"In him we have redemption through his blood, the forgiveness of sins, in accordance with the riches of God's grace that he lavished on us with all wisdom and understanding" (Ephesians 1:7,8).

3. Repent, declaring your desire to turn away from wanting to sin to wanting to obey God. It is the act of repentance that validates our confession.

"Godly sorrow brings repentance that leads to salvation and leaves no regret, but worldly sorrow brings death" (2 Corinthians 7:10).

Step 2—Not Perfect; Just Forgiven (15 Minutes)

Instruct participants to form groups of no more than five or six in each group. Assign each group one of the following incidents or stories. If there are more than four groups, assign the same passages to several groups.

Luke 7:40-50
Luke 15:1-7
Luke 18:9-14
Luke 19:1-10

Make sure each group has at least one Bible. Instruct the groups to read their passage, then discuss these questions:

If God's intent is to see people renounce sin and become obedient, why does He forgive instead of inflicting punishment on those who confess?

When a person has been forgiven, how likely is he or she to quickly return to that same sin? Why?

Why is God always willing to listen to a prayer of confession?

How often should a person ask forgiveness?

After five or six minutes of reading and discussion, invite volunteers to share insights gained from the group interaction. Be sure the following points are made:

- God's acts of forgiveness are the result of His loving-kindness, not a response we deserve or have earned.
- Many people tend to look askance at forgiveness, feeling it is a mushy, wishy-washy response when punishment should be meted out instead. There is a fear that forgiving people will just result in repeat offenses. However, such a view forgets the terrible price that Jesus paid to bring forgiveness. It also fails to recognize the transforming power at work within the person who has received forgiveness in Christ (see 2 Peter 1:3-5).
- Forgiveness should be asked for as soon as a person becomes aware of having

sinned. No one should allow unconfessed sin to remain as a barrier to fellowship with God.

Ask **What responses were evident on the part of those forgiven?** (Rejoicing, change of behavior) **In light of the rich benefits which come to those who confess, why are we so often reluctant to do so?**

After people share their thoughts on these questions, encourage them to make specific and thoughtful confession a regular part of their prayer lives.

Option: Practicing Confession

This option will add 5 minutes to the Step 2 section.

Distribute blank index cards to everyone, along with pencils for those who need them. **In order to focus your prayers of confession, take a piece of paper and a pencil and make a list of sinful attitudes and actions for which you need forgiveness. Most of us could probably use larger cards, but in a few quick moments, just write down several items that come to your mind. You will not be asked to share these.**

After two minutes, invite people to think about the items they have written. **Let's take a few moments to privately confess those actions and attitudes we know are not pleasing to God. Recoginize the price Christ paid for your sins through His death and resurrection.** Allow time for people to pray silently; then pass one or more wastebaskets around the room, inviting each person to tear up his or her card and toss the pieces into the trash, symbolizing that those sins which have been confessed have been forgiven.

Note: If you are completing this session in one meeting, ignore this break and continue with Step 3.

Two-Meeting Track: If you want to spread this session over two meetings, STOP here and close in prayer. Inform group members that your next meeting will focus on forgiveness in human relationships—forgiving others and accepting forgiveness from others.

Start Option: But You Don't Know What He Did To Me! (10 Minutes)

Before people arrive, draw a straight, horizontal line from one end of the chalkboard to the other. Across the top of the board, letter "Insult and Indignity Index." At the far left end of the line letter a large zero (0). At the far right end of the line, letter a large ten (10). Have pieces of chalk ready for people to use.

Begin your second meeting by welcoming people to the session, calling their attention to the chalkboard, and inviting them to recall a time when someone mistreated or offended them. People then go to the chalkboard and letter a one to four word description (i.e., "Spread Lies," "Cheated," "Broke Promise," etc.) of the offense they thought of, placing it somewhere between the zero (no damage done) and the ten (major damage incurred).

After a number of offenses have been added to the board, invite everyone to be seated. Read aloud the items on the board. Ask volunteers to share likely responses of someone on the receiving end of such actions.

After several comments, assign four people to read aloud one of the following passages about our response to someone who has offended us.

- Proverbs 24:17,18
- Matthew 5:43-48
- Romans 12:17-21
- 1 Peter 3:8,9

Then comment that the rest of this session will focus on what Scripture says our responses should be when we have been offended. Then continue with Step 3 and conclude the session.

Step 3—Steps to Forgiving Others (15 Minutes)

Invite everyone to look again at the prayer Jesus taught in Matthew 6. Ask a volunteer to once again read aloud Matthew 6:12: "Forgive us our debts, as we also have forgiven our debtors." Then have everyone look at verses 14 and 15 as you read Jesus' words explaining the linkage between asking for God's forgiveness and willingness to forgive others: **"For if you forgive men when they sin against you, your heavenly Father will also forgive you. But if you do not forgive men their sins, your Father will not forgive your sins" (Matthew 6:14,15). Clearly, Jesus meant for us to understand that praying for God to forgive us must also address the very common feelings of animosity and resentment we tend to harbor towards those who have offended us.**

Ask for four volunteers to take part in a brief drama of a famous story Jesus told about forgiving others. Give each volunteer, and everyone in the audience, a copy of "The Unmerciful Servant Melodrama" on page 00, and assign parts. Point out the places where audience participation is required.

After this enactment of Jesus' story, ask the following questions of the group. Encourage participants to share their thoughts, adding comments as necessary to clarify or expand on key ideas.

Why do you think Jesus' story had the king impose such a severe penalty? (The king is obviously representing God [see Matthew 18:35], and the story starkly portrays two essential aspects of God's nature: His loving-kindness and mercy in originally forgiving the debt, and His perfect justice and righteousness in punishing the wrongdoer. The seriousness of the penalty obviously reflects God's evaluation of the seriousness of the offense.)

Why do you think the penalty for not forgiving the other servant was more severe than the penalty would have been for not repaying the money owed? (Partly, it reflects the greater responsibility of the person who has received goodness from God. Also, by not forgiving the second servant, the first servant had caused damage to another. Forgiveness is consistently seen in Scripture as the means to redemption. By not offering forgiveness to another, that opportunity is denied. Just before presenting this story, Matthew reported Jesus' denouncement of anyone contributing to another person's sin [see Matthew 18:6]. It also reflects a heart attitude that despises the generosity of God—the exact opposite of a heart attitude which has truly received forgiveness.)

In light of Jesus' stern warning in verse 35, what should be a major concern for all of us whenever we ask God's forgiveness? (Obviously, we should be asking for God's help in showing His loving forgiveness to others.)

Option: Overcome Evil with Good

This option will add 5 minutes to the Step 3 section.

Instruct one third of the group to look up and read Romans 12:17,18, another third to read Romans 12:19-21, while the other third reads Matthew 5:23,24. Allow a few moments for people to locate and read their assigned passages, then ask **What do these verses add to your understanding of forgiving others?**

Step 4 Option: Seeking Forgiveness From Others (10 Minutes)

Introduce this segment with a brief comment: **Many people find that one of the most difficult things to do is to seek forgiveness from others. They feel that forgiving someone else is often much easier than asking to be forgiven.**

Ask a group member to read aloud Matthew 5:23-26, then ask these questions. Be prepared to interact about the answers to clarify the points below.

In the situation Jesus describes, who is the offender? (You, the person who is worshiping)

What does this passage indicate regarding sinful thoughts or attitudes of which the other person is unaware? (Nothing. The passage only deals with an offense which is known to the other party. Sinful thoughts which are not known to others should be confessed only to God. Obviously, if an action has been taken with the potential to hurt the other person, restitution is necessary.)

Why does Jesus indicate that forgiveness should be sought before continuing with worship? (Our worship is empty if we are aware of having offended someone without confessing it. Remind group members that the scope of our confessions need only be the scope of our offenses)

Share the following tips for asking forgiveness of someone:

- Admit to yourself and to God that what you did was wrong, without presenting any alibis or spreading any blame.
- Ask God to help you forgive the other party for anything he or she did that was wrong.
- If at all possible, arrange a face-to-face meeting with the offended person so that you can make a verbal confession. If the wrong you committed involved immorality, ask a pastor or counselor to be with you when you ask forgiveness.
- Simply and briefly admit your wrong without going into details, mitigating circumstances or attempted justifications.

- Conclude by asking, "Will you forgive me?"
- If the other person is unable to offer forgiveness, avoid the tendency to criticize or complain. Not everyone is ready to offer quick forgiveness, especially if the offense was serious.
- Whatever the outcome, pray again, thanking God for His forgiveness.

Getting Personal
(10 minutes)

Give each person a blank piece of paper, a pencil or pen, and a Bible if needed. Instruct everyone to turn to Psalm 51. Remind the group that this Psalm is attributed to King David, as he asked forgiveness after the prophet Nathan confronted him about his murder of Uriah and adultery with Bathsheba. Instruct each person to write a personalized version of the first four verses. Instead of terms such as "transgressions," "iniquity," or "sin," people are to insert specific actions or attitudes for which they need forgiveness. Be prepared to read a verse or two which you had written as a sample. Assure people that they will not need to share these verses with anyone.

After people have had time for writing, encourage them to silently and privately read the verses they just wrote. Then ask these questions:

What was difficult about putting specific, personal sins into the psalm?

Why is it often hard to admit to very specific sinful acts or feelings?

What was your reaction to reading this Psalm which identified at least one or two sins in your own life?

Encourage people to follow Jesus' model prayer by regularly confessing sins and asking forgiveness.

Getting Personal Option: Prayers of Confession

This option will add 5 minutes to the Getting Personal section.

Take a few moments to join in prayers of confession. I will mention some areas of life. Think for a few moments of any actions or attitudes about which you need forgiveness, then pray silently about each one. Mention some or all of these as areas about which to pray:

- Family Life
- Work
- Finances
- Attitude
- Spiritual Life
- Personal Relationships
- Use of Time
- Private Thoughts

Conclude the time of prayer.

Before participants leave, announce **The next session will focus on praying about temptations, and dealing with the people and forces in our lives that pull us away from God's best.**

Confused About Forgiveness?

These six prayers are all mixed up!

The first phrase of each verse is in column A, but the second phrase continues somewhere in column B, the third phrase in column C, the fourth phrase in column D and the last phrase in column E.

Draw lines to correctly connect the phrases to complete each verse.

	A	B	C	D	E
1. Numbers 14:19	In accordance with	because we are righteous	forgive	you hear,	O Lord, forgive!
2. 2 Chronicles 6:21	Hear from heaven,	not pardon	my offenses	the sin	my sins?
3. Job 7:21	Why do you	your great love,	Forgive	Lord, listen!	though it is great.
4. Psalm 19:12	Who can discern	of your name, O Lord,	but because of your great mercy.	my hidden	faults.
5. Psalm 25:11	For the sake	his errors?	forgive	and forgive	of these people.
6. Daniel 9:18, 19	We do not make requests of you	your dwelling place;	and when	my iniquity,	forgive.

What impressions about forgiveness do you gain from these prayers?

The Unmerciful Servant Melodrama
Matthew 18:21-35

Players:
King   Steward   Servant 1   Servant 2

Scene 1: The King's Work Room

The king is seated at a table, poring over an impressive stack of papers—including this script)

Steward: (Enters, carrying an impressive sheaf of papers—including this script) Your Majesty!

King: (Not looking up) Yes, yes. What is it?

Steward: Your majesty! I have found the discrepancy in your financial records!

Audience: (Applause and cheers)

King: (Now looking up) Wonderful! What was the problem?

Steward: Last year you loaned a rather large sum to one of your servants. He had persuaded you he knew a sure thing to turn a substantial profit.

Audience: (Groans)

King: I remember. Something about derivatives or stock futures or such.

Audience: (Groans louder)

King: So how much did we make on that transaction?

Steward: That's the problem, your majesty. The servant has never repaid the loan.

Audience: Boo-oo!

King: That's outrageous. Bring that scoundrel here immediately!

Steward: I have him waiting just outside the door, your Majesty. (Turns away from king and shouts.) Send in the scoundrel…I mean the servant!

Servant #1: (Enters, head down, carrying a checkbook—and this script.)

Audience: Boo-oo!

King: So, Servant #1! What do you have to say for yourself? I demand immediate repayment of... (To Steward) How much did you say I loaned him?

Steward: Ten thousand talents!

King: How much is that in real money?

Steward: Millions of dollars!

Audience: Ooo-ooh!

King: (To Servant) I order you to pay back every cent you borrowed immediately, or I'll have you and your family sold into slavery as well as everything you own!

Servant #1: Oh, please, please, your Majesty! (Holds up checkbook) I don't have the money now. But give me just a little time. I'll raise the money somehow! Pretty please!

King: (To Steward) How much will we recover by selling this poor wretch and his family and belongings?

Steward: Perhaps a few hundred dollars. A thousand tops.

King: Hardly seems worth the effort and misery. (To Servant #1) I'll tell you what. Forget the debt. I'll write it off. You're free to go.

Audience: (Applause and cheers!)

Servant #1: Thank you! Thank you! Oh, thank you!

Scene 2: A Nearby Hallway

Servant #1: (Still carrying checkbook—and this script) Wow! What a load off my mind! (Looks at checkbook) But I still don't have any money. There's gotta be a way.

Servant #2: (Enters carrying nothing—except this script) Hi, Number 1. How're things?

Servant #1: Not bad. By the way, you haven't paid me back that hundred denarii I loaned you.

Audience: Ooo-ooh.

Servant #2: How much is that in real money?

Servant #1: A couple of bucks. But I need it now. C'mon, pay up!

Audience: Boo!

Servant #2: I haven't got it on me. I'll bring it tomorrow. I promise!

Servant #1: Not good enough. You're going to jail, buddy, until you pay what you owe.

The Unmerciful Servant Melodrama

Scene 3: Back in the King's Work Room

King: (Seated at table, tossing stack of papers into waste basket—except this script) What's all that commotion out there?

Steward: (Enters, dragging Servant #1 by the arm—the one not holding this script) Your Majesty! This ungrateful scoundrel, the one you forgave of a huge debt, has just had another servant sent to jail for owing him just a few dollars!

Audience: Boo! Hiss!

Servant #1: Well, I needed the money to buy lunch.

King: (Standing up majestically) Silence! You wicked servant! I cancelled all that debt of yours because you begged me to. Shouldn't you have had mercy on your fellow servant just as I had on you? (Angrily) Take him away! Lock him up until every penny is paid back!

Steward: This way, scoundrel!

Lead Us Not Into Temptation

Session Keys

Key Verse
"And lead us not into temptation, but deliver us from the evil one." Matthew 6:13

Key Idea
God offers His great power to protect His people from temptation and sin.

Background

A world in which all our choices were obvious would be so much easier to handle than all the ambiguous issues which confront us in real life. If only everything were clearly black or clearly white, instead of various shades of gray, then making the right decisions would not be so difficult.

But the world is not all black or all white, so every day we face situations in which the good and right option is not clearly obvious. The story of Jesus' temptations reveals that many things can look very good to us, but be very evil instead. Rational arguments can be put forth, justifying that which is unjust, defending that which is destructive. Very subtly, but very powerfully, as we allow ourselves to focus on the attractive aspects, we are drawn as into a magnetic field, increasingly unable to resist the allure of something very dangerous. Even when we recognize the face of evil in that which attracts us, the power of the temptation is not lessened.

Jesus, as someone who had been "tempted in every way, just as we are" (Hebrews 4:15), knew full well the powerful pull of temptation. Jesus had not lightly flicked away temptation. He had not found it easy to overcome. Instead, "because he himself suffered when he was tempted, he is able to help those who are being tempted" (Hebrews 2:18).

Imagine the perfect Son of God suffering while being tempted! If Jesus struggled to make the right choice and to withstand the pressures to do what was popular, is it any wonder we also find it difficult to discern what is right and then choose to do it? No wonder Jesus taught us to to ask for God's deliverance in our imperfect struggles to resist the lure with which Satan desires to hook us.

The second half of this session deals with the process of prayer, looking at both how Jesus prayed and when and where He prayed. It is more than an interesting feature of His life that Jesus, the Son of God, found it necessary to spend time alone with His heavenly Father. Rather than letting the business of His days—days filled with traveling, speaking to crowds, healing the sick, answering questions and teaching His disciples—distract Him from prayer, we consistently see Jesus setting aside time to be alone with God.

Just as healthy food is necessary for our bodies to produce the cells and hormones needed for life, so we also need spiritual nourishment. Input from God's Word and fellowship through prayer are essential for spiritual growth. A day or two without prayer or Bible reading may not cause any noticeable problems, but if prayerlessness and neglect of Scriptures become habits, we gradually stop growing and begin stagnating without the benefit of God's wisdom for the daily challenges of living.

Preparation

- Provide blank name tags and felt-tip pens. Make a tag for yourself.
- On a table at the front of the room, provide materials for one of these Getting Started choices:
  - Choice 1: Talk About Temptation—Provide a large sheet of newsprint and several felt-tip pens for each group of four to six people. Also have a roll of masking tape available. On an extra sheet of paper, letter this slogan in large letters: "You can't stop birds from flying over your head, but you can keep them from building a nest in your hair." Mount the paper on a wall of the room.
  - Choice 2: I Tend To Give In When...—Duplicate copies of "I Tend To Give In When..." on page 81, providing one copy per person. Provide pens or pencils for those who need them.
  - Option: Temptation Trivia—A chalkboard and chalk, or an overhead projector, blank transparency and a transparency pen.
- Make a copy of "Praying to Make Right Choices" on page 83 for each participant.
- Write Colossians 1:9-14 on a sheet of paper, inserting the names of your group members throughout the text so that it reads as a prayer for each of them. For example: "For this reason,... I am praying for (Jim Smith) and asking God to fill (Vicky Brown) with the knowledge of his will (and for Manuel Gomez) through all spiritual wisdom and understanding...."
- On three separate sheets of poster board, letter these "quotes," putting the first part of a quote on one side, and the rest of the quote on the back side of the poster:
  "Yield not to temptation—but yielding is fun."
  "Get thee behind me, Satan—and push."
  "I was sinking deep in sin—Whee-ee!"
- Provide blank writing paper and pencils or pens for each participant.

Session 4 at a Glance

SECTION	ONE-SESSION PLAN		TWO-SESSION PLAN	WHAT YOU'LL DO
Time Schedule	60 to 75 Minutes	More than 75 Minutes	60 Minutes (each session)	
Getting Started	10	10-20	20	Get Acquainted—Introduce Topic of Temptation
Getting into the Word	40	60-75	40	
Step 1 Praying To Make Right Choices	10	20	20	Examine Scriptures Dealing with Temptation
Step 2 Wanting to Do What We Know Is Right	15	20	20	Learn Ways to See Right as More Appealing Than Wrong
			Session 2 Start Option: 10	
Step 3 Learning to Listen, Not Just Talk	10	20	20	Explore the Benefits of Conversational Prayer
(Step 4 Option) Personal Quiet Time	(10)	(10)	15	Consider Eight Tips for Spending Daily Time with God
Getting Personal	10	10-15	15	Spend Time in Prayer

Session Plan

Leader's Choice

Two-Meeting Track: This session is designed to be completed in one 60- to 75-minute meeting. If you want to extend the session over two meetings and allow group members more time for discussion, **END** your first meeting and **BEGIN** your second meeting at the stop-and-go symbol in the session plan.

The boxes marked with the clock symbol provide optional learning experiences to extend this session over two meetings or to accommodate a session longer than 60-75 minutes.

Getting Started
(10 minutes)

Choice 1—Talk About Temptation

Welcome people as they arrive and suggest they make and wear name tags. Ask participants to form groups of no more than six people and work together to write a slogan for an advertising campaign to "tempt" (influence, entice, stimulate) people to resist temptation. Refer to the sample slogan you lettered. Encourage the groups to be creative, thinking of catchy or thoughtful ways to phrase advice about not giving in when tempted.

As groups finish their slogans, have them mount them on the walls of the room. Ask volunteers to read aloud the slogans they wrote. Then ask **Being hard-nosed realists, how effective do you think any of our slogans would be in keeping someone from giving in to the strong pull of temptation?** After several people respond, lead into the rest of the session with this comment: **Slogans and good advice may be helpful at times, but today we are going to explore the most reliable approach available to protect us from our very human tendencies to be drawn into attitudes and actions we know are wrong.**

Choice 2—I Tend To Give In When...

Welcome people as they arrive and suggest they make and wear name tags. Give each person a copy of the "I Tend To Give In When..." page, and a pen or pencil, if needed. Encourage each person to complete each of the statements on the page, identifying situations and factors which tend to make them more susceptible than usual to temptations. Tell them **The purpose is not to get someone to reveal deep, personal struggles, but to help us all to think of the times, places and situations in which we may tend to give in to something we know we shouldn't. Complete your own page as others work on theirs.**

After several minutes in which people think and write, read aloud two or three completions from your paper. Then invite volunteers to each read one or two from their pages. After several have shared, introduce this session's topic by commenting: **We all know the pull of temptation, and all of us have certain temptations to which we are susceptible. In this session we will explore Jesus' instruction to pray for God's protection against those temptations.**

Getting Started Option: Temptation Trivia

This option will add 10 minutes to the Getting Started section.

After completing one of the Getting Started activities, say **There are many stories in Scripture of people who were tempted. Some gave in to the temptation, others resisted. We're going to have a little competition here to see which side of the room can think of the most stories about temptation.** Divide the room in half. Draw

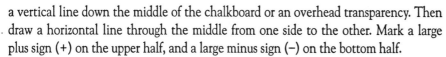
a vertical line down the middle of the chalkboard or an overhead transparency. Then draw a horizontal line through the middle from one side to the other. Mark a large plus sign (+) on the upper half, and a large minus sign (−) on the bottom half.

Invite volunteers on one side of the room to identify someone in Scripture who successfully resisted temptation (i.e., Jesus, Joseph, Daniel, Esther, etc.). When a name is called out, write it in the plus section on that side of the chart. Then ask the other side to identify someone who gave in to temptation (Adam, Eve, David, Peter, Achan, Saul, etc.). Write that person's name in the minus section of the other side of the chart. Continue similarly, alternating so that one time a team tries to think of someone on the plus side, and the next time on the minus side.

As soon as one team is unable to answer (or starts coming up with very unlikely ideas), interject this comment: **Obviously, a lot of people in the Bible were tempted. And thinking of people who successfully resisted temptation is usually more difficult than recalling people who gave in. Fortunately, we are not helpless against temptation's powers.**

Ask a volunteer to read aloud Hebrews 2:17,18, a powerfully reassuring passage about the help we have through Christ to remain faithful in the face of temptation. This assurance forms the basis of the study in this session.

Getting into the Word
(40 minutes)

Step 1—Praying to Make Right Choices (10 Minutes)

Introduce this topic by reading aloud Matthew 6:13: "And lead us not into temptation, but deliver us from the evil one." Add this comment: **It is significantly interesting that in this brief prayer, almost half of the text deals with the problem of evil. First, the prayer for forgiveness deals with sinful actions and attitudes which have already occurred. Then, in verse 13, Jesus teaches us to ask for help in avoiding sins which have not yet been committed. We're going to look at some very clear statements about the help God provides in making right choices and not giving in to temptation.**

Instruct people to form groups of no more than six in each group. Distribute copies of the "Praying to Make Right Choices" page, along with pencils or pens, if needed. Assign each group one of the four Scripture passages on the page. They are to read their assigned text, then discuss with each other what their passage adds to their understanding of how to deal with the temptations which confront them. After three or four minutes, invite volunteers from each group to share the insights they gained about dealing with temptation. Be prepared to clarify or expand on their comments, if needed.

1 Corinthians 10:13

- We need not worry that we will be victimized by some overpowering temptation that no one else has ever faced.

- We can depend on God to ensure that no temptation will be too great for us.
- The promise is *not* that we will never be tempted, but that God will enable us to resist and overcome.

Hebrews 2:18-3:1
- Jesus offers us the same help which enabled Him to triumph, even through temptation strong enough to cause Him very real suffering.
- When we are tempted, our assistance comes when we focus on Christ, not on the temptation.

Hebrews 4:15, 16
- Again, we have the successful example of Jesus' triumph over sin.
- Jesus does not condemn us for the struggles we endure because of our weaknesses. Instead, He sympathizes with our struggles.
- Gaining access into the very presence of God does not demand that we achieve perfection. We are not required to achieve perfection by triumphing over all temptation. Instead, because of Jesus, we can confidently approach God when we are in the midst of the struggle, asking for His help.
- When we fail, we are not banished. Nor do we encounter accusations and denunciations. Instead we find grace and mercy.

James 1:13-15
- Temptation does not come from God. Nor can it all be blamed on Satan, even though he certainly is involved in the process. Temptation succeeds because of our own selfish desires.
- Temptation is not a sin. But to give into temptation is sin. Even though temptations always look appealing at the time, the end result is ultimately spiritual death.

To summarize this discussion, ask **Therefore, when we are tempted to do something wrong, what is the one action these verses all indicate we should take in order to ensure that we will make the right choice instead.** (Obviously, pray about it.)

Option: Paul's Prayer for the Colossians

This option will add 10 minutes to the Step 1 section.

Ask a group member to read Colossians 1:9-14 aloud, encouraging people to follow along and note the ways Paul's prayers address the need for help in resisting temptation. When the reading is completed, invite volunteers to call out the requests Paul made and tell how these requests aid in overcoming temptation. Be prepared to add clarifying comments, if needed:

- "fill you with the knowledge of his will" (v. 9)—the better we know God and understand His purposes, the more we will be drawn to do what is right and stay away from that which detracts from His objectives;
- "that you may live a life worthy of the Lord and may please him in every way" (v. 10) describes a positive pattern of life in which temptation is being overcome;
- "bearing fruit...growing...being strengthened...great endurance and patience"

(vv. 10,11) are just some descriptions in these verses of the spiritually healthy person who has been enabled to resist the lure of evil;

- "he has rescued us from the dominion of darkness...redemption, the forgiveness of sins" (vv. 13,14) are the only direct references in this passage to the problems caused by evil.

Clearly, the emphasis in Paul's prayer is not on the threats posed by evil, but on the person and work of Christ. Temptation is defeated, not by focusing on the dangers, but on the Deliverer.

Read the Colossians passage aloud again, making it a prayer for the people in your group with their names inserted throughout the text.

Step 2—Wanting to Do What We Know is Right (15 Minutes)

Once we realize that prayer gives us access to all the knowledge and strength we need, we must ask ourselves, "So, why don't we pray every time temptation comes our way?" Accept suggestions from group members, then say **Our failure to claim God's help when we face temptation may be related to some long-standing attempts at humor that most of you have probably heard at some time or another.** Hold up the first poster you prepared, showing the quote, "Yield not to temptation—." Then show the back side: "but yielding is fun." Repeat similarly with the other two posters. Some people will laugh; others may be offended; some may simply be surprised that you dared to share those "jokes" in church.

Comment: **These posters illustrate what is usually the real reason we don't start praying the moment we face a temptation to sin. Our problem isn't _knowing_ whether something is right or wrong. Our problem is _not wanting_ to do the right thing rather than the wrong thing. Something within us wants to taste the forbidden fruit, for we fear we might miss out on something. Thus, we not so secretly wish that Satan would get behind us and push, so that we could be relieved of the responsibility, even as we indulge in what we know is wrong. We'd like to be able to defend ourselves later by claiming, "The devil made me do it."**

Therefore, the crucial question for all of us is, how can we consistently _want_ to do what we know is right and resist the pull to do what is wrong? Let's look at three passages which address this question:

Before you read aloud Psalm 1:1-3, ask one third of the group to listen for what a person should _not_ do, have another third listen for what a person _should_ do, and the last third listen for the _result_ of doing the right thing. Read the three verses aloud, then invite volunteers from each section to share the response to their assignment:

1. Do not participate in the sinful activities of those who do not follow God. The basic idea is stated slightly different three times, a device used for emphasis:
   walk—refers to the pattern of conducting life's affairs; not merely being in company with the ungodly, but acting "in synch" with them
   counsel—their ideas, advice, manner of thinking
   stand—position yourself, identify with
   sit—to settle in, become comfortable

2. Do consistently look to God for guidance in all areas of life. Rather than hoping for pleasure among the ungodly people and activities of this world, we are to discover the pure joy that only comes from living God's way.

3. The results are strength, success and productivity, which benefits not only the individual, but also others. How often do we observe someone seeking "personal fulfillment," whose quest "feels" good for a time, but leaves a wake of damage and brokenness?

Next, point out that Isaiah 64:5-9 expresses awareness of the help God provides, as well as the tendency for people to sin in spite of that. Encourage people to notice the vivid descriptions of what sin brings to a life, and the relationship between God and His imperfect people. It also raises the vital question, "How then can we be saved?" Then read the verses aloud.

Ask, **Who did the passage say God will help?** (He will help "those who gladly do right, who remember your ways" [v. 5]. This is another description of the person whose "delight is in the law of the Lord" [Psalm 1:2].)

Why is it important to have a realistic view of sin and its results? (Satan attempts to deceive us, getting us to focus on what seems attractive about a course of action. From the time of Adam and Eve, people have succumbed to temptation without considering the deadly result. When we realize, as the writer of this passage, what sin really produces, we will be much less likely to be drawn to it.)

What is the nature of our relationship with God? And how does awareness of that relationship help us avoid being drawn into sin? (When we sin, God is described as being angry, and as withdrawing from contact with us. He is described as our Father—one of the relatively few Old Testament references which do so—and as the Potter who forms the clay. In verse 9 is the recognition "for we are all your people." Sin is most likely to gain the upper hand when we envision God as far removed, even disinterested in our lives. In contrast, when we focus on His concern for us, His personal interest in us, the response is to want to please Him, not to disobey Him.)

Ask someone in the group to read aloud Philippians 4:8,9. Point out the obvious emphasis on the importance of intentionally choosing to focus our thoughts on that which is good. Remember the old computer jargon: Garbage in, garbage out. **The things we let our minds dwell on—what we choose to read, to watch, to listen to—have a big impact on our resulting behavior.** Notice the progression of Paul's instructions here:

1. Intentionally focus thoughts on what is good.
2. Practice doing what you have been taught.
3. God will be with you.

Notice, God does not control our thoughts, or force us to want to do right. But once we take a step toward Him, He is always ready to respond, bringing us the joy and satisfaction which comes from doing what is good.

Option: Prayer For God's Help

This option will add 5 minutes to the Step 2 section.

Let's take some time to pray for God's help in wanting to do right. Invite volunteers to suggest some of the good, true, admirable things in life for which to thank God and focus our thoughts on. As each one is mentioned, have a few moments of silent, prayerful thought about why that is praiseworthy. Conclude with a request for God's help in continuing to focus on those things, gaining delight from God's Word and living God's way.

Note: If you are completing this session in one meeting, ignore this break and continue with Step 3.

Two-Track Meeting: If you want to spread this session over two meetings, STOP here and close in prayer. Inform group members that your next meeting will focus on specific approaches in prayer which people will find helpful.

Start Option: Helpful and Difficult (10 Minutes)

Begin your second meeting by inviting group members to share what they find helpful about their times of prayer and what they find difficult. As comments are shared, list them on the chalkboard or an overhead transparency under the columns "Helpful" or "Difficult." As each item is listed, ask for a show of hands of those who share that person's experience, finding the same things helpful or difficult.

Then invite volunteers to share any ways in which the time spent in this class has aided in making prayer more helpful and/or less difficult. After several have commented, continue with Step 3 and conclude the session.

Step 3—Learning to Listen, Not Just Talk (15 Minutes)

Ask **How many of you have ever found yourself having a hard time leaving a message on an answering machine?** Most people are likely to raise their hand. Then ask, **Why do we often find it harder to talk to a machine than to a live person?** Answers may include:

- There is no interaction.
- You're not sure if, or when, the message will be heard.
- It just feels more impersonal even if the other person is someone you know well.

Somewhat similar to the problem most of us have at times with answering machines, many people find prayer difficult because it is hard for them to focus on the Person to whom their prayers are addressed. Not being able to see God, or hear His responses to the things said in prayer, contributes to some people finding their mind wandering, their concentration wavering. Let's take a few minutes to consider an approach to praying that many people have found helpful, especially during group prayer times, in overcoming these problems. This approach is called conversational prayer.

Ask **What benefits would be likely from prayer that is phrased more like a nor-

mal conversation and less like a speech? Answers people suggest are likely to include:

- It can feel more like talking personally with God, without need for formalities that can create feelings of distance.
- Everyone has a lifetime of experience with informal conversation, thus a conversational approach to prayer is familiar, reducing awkwardness for many people.
- Learning to think of God as our loving, heavenly Father opens the door to an intimacy of relationship.
- In group prayer situations, a conversational approach reduces the pressure to create an "impressive" prayer, allowing people to be more honest and direct.
- Groups which practice conversational-style prayer find that it is easier for people to concentrate on, and to mentally and spiritually join in with each other's prayers than if group members offer a series of lengthier, more formal prayers.

After several benefits have been mentioned, present the following guidelines for using conversational prayer in a group:

- Use only informal, conversational language. Avoid archaic terms and "Christian jargon" which tend to make many people feel they are making a speech rather than talking to their loving, heavenly Father.
- Address only one topic or concern in any single prayer. Just as in a dialog or group conversation, no polite person would monopolize the discussion by declaiming on a series of topics without allowing others to interject their thoughts and feelings, or to suggest other topics. This guideline avoids having anyone launch into a lengthy recitation of issues which may or may not be of concern to the rest of the group.
- Before anyone raises a new topic, at least one person should agree in prayer about the issue raised in the previous person's prayer. Thus, if the first person to pray asks for strength to avoid a particular temptation, the next person to pray should respond to that request, as a participant in an ongoing, considerate conversation. Then the third person is free to also address that same concern, or to raise a new topic. This guideline nudges people to show the conversational courtesy of acknowledging what someone else has said, not just abruptly changing the subject at whim. It also encourages group members to be thinking along with the person who is praying, rather than just organizing their thoughts for what they want to pray about as soon as they get a turn. Actually listening to, and then also praying for, what others pray about is a very helpful way to allow prayer to be a two-way communication instead of just a monolog in which we talk and God listens.

Ask **What are some other ways to open our prayer experiences so that we are receptive to allowing God to speak to us?** Accept ideas from group members, and be prepared to share one or more of these:

- Interweave praying with reading from Scripture. For example, specifically ask God to help you learn from His Word, then read a few verses, then pray about what you have just read.
- When in prayer, ask God to help you be open to what He wants you to know and to do regarding the matter about which you are praying. **Caution:** The next idea to pop into your head is not necessarily from God. But, over time, as you pray, listen and read His Word, you will become able to discern when your thoughts are in accord with His purposes.
- Sing a hymn or worship chorus, then meditate on the message. **Caution:** Be cautious about getting your theology out of the hymn book, rather than out of the Bible.

Option: Thees and Thous and Thys

This option will add 5 minutes to the Step 3 section.

Take a few moments to deal with the question of the style of pronouns used in addressing God. Many people feel that using "Thou," "Thee," "Thy" and "Thine" are forms of respect for God's greatness and holiness. This opinion about these forms is relatively recent, and was not the intent in their usage several hundred years ago, such as when the *King James Version* of the Bible was translated. At that time, "thou" was used in day-to-day conversation when addressing a person with whom the speaker was intimate: a child, a family member, a household servant or a social inferior. When used in addressing God, the intent was to convey a close, personal relationship. In the familiar *King James Version* rendering of the opening of the Lord's Prayer "Our Father which art in heaven, hallowed be thy name," the use of "thy" is in keeping with a close parent-child relationship with God the Father, not emphasizing a sense of reverence for His exalted status. The pronoun "you," which was originally a plural pronoun, had gradually become used in polite address to a single person, especially when that person was a stranger or someone of higher social status. In the intervening years, "thou" has ceased being used in day-to-day conversation (except in a few dialects), but has continued to be part of many people's "prayer language." To the extent that people understand the actual meaning of "thou," its usage can add a rich texture of intimacy to prayer. But for many for whom it simply sounds archaic, it actually inhibits their sense of closeness to God, making Him seem distant, as well as out of date. Thus, in conversational group prayer at least, it is usually best for everyone to address God using the ordinary and friendly pronouns "you" and "yours."

Step 4 Option—Personal Quiet Time (10 Minutes)

Read aloud 1 Peter 2:2,3: **"Like newborn babies, crave pure spiritual milk, so that by it you may grow up in your salvation, now that you have tasted that the Lord is good."** Comment: **Just as our physical bodies require food on a regular, consistent basis, so does our spiritual nature require continuing, reliable nourishment. We're going to consider eight tips for gaining that needed input through a rich, rewarding** prayer time on a regular basis. Present a brief lecture of these eight suggestions:

1. Set aside a regular time each day to spend in prayer. People with busy schedules never "find" time; we have to make time. Some people choose morning as a way to get the right start on each day. The key is to choose a time when you are alert.

2. Set aside a regular place for your Quiet Time. Mark 1:35 tells us that Jesus found a "solitary" place for His Quiet Time.

3. Use a notebook to record significant aspects of each Quiet Time:
    *   Prayer requests and answers;
    *   Insights from reading the Word;
    *   Attitudes before, during, and after Quiet Time.

4. Begin with praise and adoration, honoring God for His deeds and for His character.

5. Confess any sin in your life, asking God to forgive and to keep you from temptation and further sin.

6. Have a plan for regular Bible reading, then read slowly and thoughtfully. The goal is not to "get through" a lot of material, but to let God speak through the verses that are read. It is better to read a few verses which you can apply to your life than many verses that remain a blur. Always ask yourself questions about how the passage applies to situations you are currently facing:
    *   How does this passage relate to my life today?
    *   Is there a promise I can claim?
    *   What response should I make to what I have read?

7. Pray about what you have read, about what is currently going on in your life and in the lives of others.

8. On occasion, vary what you do in your Quiet Times:
    *   Write your prayer as a letter to God;
    *   Personalize the passage you are reading, inserting your own name and situation into the verses;
    *   Interweave Bible reading with prayer, reading a verse or phrase, then responding to what it said with an expression of praise or a request;
    *   Switch your Quiet Time to a different place and/or time, especially if your schedule changes and your usual routine will not work;
    *   Take a few moments to memorize a verse or two and then think about it throughout the day;
    *   Read the Bible aloud. (The Bible was originally written to be heard.)

Getting Personal

(10 minutes)

Invite participants to form groups of no more than four or five people. We are going

to spend the next five to seven minutes together in conversational prayer for avoiding temptation and for growth in our spiritual lives. Remind the group of the guidelines for conversational prayer within a group:

- Use only informal, conversational language.
- Address only one topic or concern in any single prayer.
- Before anyone raises a new topic, at least one person should also pray about the issue raised in the previous person's prayer.

Join one of the groups as people pray together. Conclude the prayer time by singing (or enlisting someone else to do so) a simple worship chorus which is familiar to your group.

Getting Personal Option: Prayer Intentions

This option will add 5 minutes to the Getting Personal section.

Instruct participants to stand and form partners or trios. While still standing, have partners share with each other one thing they intend to do in their personal prayer times during the coming week. Then have partners conclude the session by praying for each other to follow through on their prayer intentions.

Before participants leave, announce **The next session will focus on praise, our expressions of gratitude for the good God does for us.**

I Tend To Give In When...

Write your completions to the following statements to describe some of the circumstances which leave you most susceptible to temptation. You need not reveal any deep, personal struggles, but do seek to identify the moments when you are most likely to "break down" and do something you know you should not do.

I tend to give in to _____
whenever...

Whenever _____ ,
I just can't resist...

I could hold out against _____
if it just weren't for...

It would be so much easier to _____
if I just didn't have to...

I know I shouldn't _____ ,
but I lose all my will power when...

Praying to Make the Right Choices

"And lead us not into temptation, but deliver us from the evil one"
(Matthew 6:13).

What do each of the following verses add to our understanding of how to deal with the temptations which confront us?

"No temptation has seized you except what is common to man. And God is faithful; he will not let you be tempted beyond what you can bear. But when you are tempted, he will also provide a way out so that you can stand up under it" (1 Corinthians 10:13).

"Because he himself [Jesus] suffered when he was tempted, he is able to help those who are being tempted. Therefore, holy brothers, who share in the heavenly calling, fix your thoughts on Jesus, the apostle and high priest whom we confess" (Hebrews 2:18–3:1).

"For we do not have a high priest who is unable to sympathize with our weaknesses, but we have one who has been tempted in every way, just as we are—yet was without sin. Let us then approach the throne of grace with confidence, so that we may receive mercy and find grace to help us in our time of need" (Hebrews 4:15,16).

"When tempted, no one should say, 'God is tempting me.' For God cannot be tempted by evil, nor does he tempt anyone; but each one is tempted when, by his own evil desire, he is dragged away and enticed. Then, after desire has conceived, it gives birth to sin; and sin, when it is full-grown, gives birth to death" (James 1:13-15).

The Kingdom and the Power and the Glory

Session Keys

Key Verse

"For yours is the kingdom and the power and the glory forever. Amen." Matthew 6:13

Key Idea

God is honored by the praises of His people.

Background

Prayer is paying attention to God. It can be easy to focus on our list of requests, our needs and anxieties. But prayer moves far beyond a recitation of personal concerns once we become aware we are speaking to the One who cares far more than we do. Conversation with God comes alive when we recognize that the God we are addressing is infinitely more powerful than our circumstances.

Do you feel far removed from God when you pray? Try praising Him. The Psalmist declares that God inhabits the praises of His people. When we praise Him, He is present with us.

Do you feel no stirrings of praise, no sense of adoration or worship? Expressing praise is a declaration of faith—a statement that God deserves our honor and respect, even when our emotions are not attuned to respond appropriately. Praising God, even when we do not feel like it, is a way to move towards experiencing the reality of what we say we believe.

We must recognize, in every prayer we offer, that God alone is ruler of the kingdoms of heaven and earth. Our prayers must be grounded in trust that He possesses all the real power and deserves all the glory because of who He is and what He has done.

We tend to think of prayer in terms of it being something we do because we are so often motivated to pray by some personal need or concern or desire. In reality, prayer actually starts with God. Just as a love letter is inspired by the person who is beloved, so God must be the inspiration of our prayer. However, because our thoughts and feelings tend to be dominated by the tangible things and people which surround us, we need to guard against our communication with God being dominated by our own desires and concerns. Thus, praise needs to be the foundation for our prayers, not because God needs to hear it, but because we need to express it. Our expressions of praise cause us to become aware that God is truly worthy.

We have a need to express what God means to us, and in this process, allow Him to remind us of the many aspects of His nature. As we praise Him, we begin to think about our life from God's perspective which is essential preparation for making requests for our own needs and those of others. As praise raises our awareness of this gracious God, we are awed by the realization that He offers us personal friendship with Himself, and that He understands our needs, even before they are spoken (see Matthew 6:8). Through praise we discover that our relationship with God is of much more value than any of the things we ask Him to give. Praise opens our eyes to the wonderful God who gives according to His own perfect purposes.

Therefore, our prayers need to be centered in our relationship with Christ. It is through Christ that God has sought to restore and build a relationship with His people. By raising Jesus from the dead, He has proven His control over both humanity and nature. And by giving us a place in His eternal kingdom, He makes His greatness personal and deserving of our eternal adoration.

Preparation

- Provide blank name tags and felt-tip pens. Make a tag for yourself.
- On a table at the front of the room, provide materials for this Getting Started choice, plus the other activities you choose to offer:
  - Choice 1: I See in You... Tape to the bottom of about one-third of the chairs different colored circles or squares, making sure no two chairs have identical shapes and colors. Place a matching set of shapes in a paper bag. Place one chair (with no shape under it) at the front of the room. If some of your people tend to arrive a little late, set aside a number of chairs without shapes to increase the likelihood that someone will be seated in the chairs with the shapes under them.
  - Getting Started Option: Exhortation to Praise—A Bible for every two or three participants.
- Letter the words of Matthew 6:13 on poster board and mount it at the front of the room.
- Letter the following phrase across the top of the chalkboard or a blank overhead transparency: "Praising God is...."
- Duplicate copies of "Praising God Is..." on page 95, providing one copy per person. Have Bibles and pencils or pens ready for those who need them.
- Make a transparency of "Praise: An Expression of Faith" on page 97. Secure an overhead projector and focus it at the front of the room.
- Provide blank writing paper and pencils for each participant.

Session 5 at a Glance

SECTION	ONE-SESSION PLAN		TWO-SESSION PLAN	WHAT YOU'LL DO
Time Schedule	60 to 75 Minutes	More than 75 Minutes	60 Minutes (each session)	
Getting Started	10	10-20	20	Experience Giving Praise to Others
Getting Into the Word	40	60-75	40	
Step 1 Praise: A Joyful Response	15	20	20	Study Scriptures About Praising God
Step 2 Praise: An Expression of Faith	10	20	20	Answer Questions About Praising God Before He Intervenes
			Session 2 Start Option: 10	
Step 3 Praise: Stirring Awareness of His Presence	15	20	20	Examine the Connection Between Praise and Faith
(Step 4 Option) When We Praise	(10)	(10)	15	Share Insights About Three Types of Praise
Getting Personal	10	10-15	15	Write a Letter of Praise to God

Session Plan

Leader's Choice

Two-Meeting Track: This session is designed to be completed in one 60- to 75-minute meeting. If you want to extend the session over two meetings and allow group members more time for discussion, **END** your first meeting and **BEGIN** your second meeting at the stop-and-go symbol in the session plan.

The boxes marked with the clock symbol provide optional learning experiences to extend this session over two meetings or to accommodate a session longer than 60-75 minutes.

Getting Started

(10 minutes)

Choice 1—I See in You...

Welcome people as they arrive and suggest they make and wear name tags. Select a shape from the paper bag you prepared and ask people to look under their chairs to see if anyone has that shape. (If not, draw other shapes from the bag until one matches a shape on the bottom of someone's chair.) Invite that "lucky" person to sit in the chair at the front of the room. Then say **Today we are going to be learning about praise, a vital part of our prayer experiences. To help us understand why praising God is so important in prayer, we are going to do a simple experiment with praising ourselves. Thus, for the next 90 seconds, we are going to shower (person at front of room) with praise, pointing out positive things we know or can observe.** Begin timing, and offer the first brief word of praise about your "volunteer." When the 90 seconds is up, draw another shape from the bag and repeat the process with another person. Continue with as many people as time allows.

Lead into the topic for the session by asking **In listening to the words of praise we offered our rather embarrassed volunteers, how many of you learned something new about at least one of these people? How many noticed something about them you might not have paid attention to otherwise?** Then point out, **Praising God is not something we do because He needs to hear it. We are the ones who need to make ourselves aware of His praiseworthiness. Our need to praise God will be the focus of this final exploration of prayer.**

Choice 2—A Complimentary Exchange

Welcome people as they arrive and suggest they make and wear name tags.

Instruct participants to mingle and ask at least three people **What was the most recent compliment you have received?** Comment (humorously) **Hopefully, none of us will have to remember too far back, and please avoid any false modesty. You all have my permission to brag a little on yourselves.**

After several minutes of interaction, invite participants to be seated. Ask volunteers to share compliments they heard someone else receive. Since many people find it difficult to give or receive compliments, mention two or three you heard people sharing. For example, **I heard Jim mention that one of his kids complimented him on the good hamburgers he barbecues. And Vicky said her neighbor complimented her on how well her garden is doing this year.** Your sharing will set an example of complimenting group members without turning it into an opportunity for friendly gibes or "back-handed" compliments.

After several people have shared, lead into the topic of praise by asking **What benefit is there in our relationships to think and talk about each other's good qual-**

ities? Those of you who told about a compliment someone else had received, how did you feel about that person as you were sharing that information? Allow several people to respond, then comment: Praising God is not something we do because He needs to hear it. We are the ones who need to make ourselves aware of His praiseworthiness. Our need to praise God will be the focus of this final exploration of prayer.

Getting Started Option: Exhortations to Praise

This option will add 10 minutes to the Getting Started section.

After completing one of the Getting Started activities, have people form pairs or trios. Assign those in each quarter of your room to read one of the following statements about praise from the book of Psalms:

Psalm 9:1,2
Psalm 33:1-4
Psalm 66:1-4
Psalm 100:4,5

Ask each pair or trio to talk about what reasons their assigned Scripture gives for praising God. After three or four minutes, invite volunteers to share what they have discussed. Write their reasons to praise on the chalkboard or an overhead transparency.

Getting into the Word

(40 minutes)

Step 1—Praise: A Joyful Response (15 Minutes)

Introduce this topic by directing attention to the poster with the concluding statement from the Lord's prayer: "For yours is the kingdom and the power and the glory forever. Amen" (Matthew 6:13). Then comment: **The earliest manuscripts of Matthew's Gospel do not include this familiar statement of praise, which recognizes the sovereignty, power, and worthiness of God. Most scholars believe the phrase was added to later manuscripts to record the common pattern of worship by believers at that time. The repeated use of the phrase over many centuries in churches around the world has made it a powerful reminder, along with many other passages of Scripture, of the importance of praise in our prayers.**

Point out the phrase on the chalkboard or overhead: "Praising God is..." Ask group members to suggest the first completion to the phrase which comes to mind (i.e., "Praising God is better than complaining," or "Praising God is recognizing His greatness."). Accept several responses, lettering them on the chalkboard or overhead.

Then distribute the "Praising God Is..." page to each person and call attention to the definition printed there: **Praising God is expressing approval, admiration, honor or reverence to Him.** Next, offer this explanation: **Christians have a God-given desire to praise and adore God. However, we have a very human tendency to for-**

get to praise Him, often because we are too busy taking the credit ourselves for the good that occurs in our lives.

Assign half of your group to read Psalm 100 while the rest of the people read Ephesians 1:3-8. Ask each person to write on the "Praising God Is..." page what that assigned Scripture says about praise. After a few minutes, invite volunteers to share insights about praise that they gained from the verses they read. Be prepared to add these points if needed:

Psalm 100:

- Praise is an expression of joy ("Shout for joy to the Lord...Worship the Lord with gladness; come before him with joyful songs" [vv. 1,2].)
- Joyful praise is the appropriate response of recognizing that God truly is God, the Creator of all, who continues to care for His people as a shepherd for His sheep.
- While we may not always feel joyful, God continues to be good and faithful and unchanging over time, always deserving of our thankful praise.

Ephesians 1:3-8:

- Praise is due to God for the spiritual benefits He has provided us.
- Our adoption into His family brings praise to God, not credit to us.
- Praise to God is the appropriate response when we consider "his glorious grace, which he has freely given us... redemption through his blood, the forgiveness of sins,...the riches of God's grace that he lavished on us with all wisdom and understanding" (vv. 6-8).

Direct attention to the next statement on the "Praising God Is..." page: "A few reasons we are to praise God:" Invite responses to this statement, then assign each of the passages listed (Psalm 28:6-9; Psalm 34:1-7; Psalm 47; Acts 3:1-10; Revelation 4:8-11) to group members in different sections of the room. Instruct them to read and identify any reasons they discover as to why we are to praise God, why we know He is worthy of our praise (see Psalm 48:1).

After several minutes, call for volunteers to share their findings. Group members will share thoughts such as:

- God is worthy of our praise, for He has done wonderful things (answered prayer, delivered out of trouble, created all things);
- God is worthy of our praise because of who He is ("awesome... the great King over all the earth...holy" [Psalm 47:2,8]);
- Scripture repeatedly instructs us to praise Him ("Glorify the Lord" [Psalm 34:3]; "Clap your hands... Sing praises to God..." [Psalm 47:1,6]);
- Praise expresses our thanks for His goodness to us. ("My heart leaps for joy and I will give thanks to him in song" [Psalm 28:7]).

Option: Was No One Found To Give Praise?

This option will add 5 minutes to the Step 1 section.

Read aloud the story of Jesus healing the ten men with leprosy (Luke 17:12-19). After reading the story, ask **How many times in our lives might God have asked,**

"Was no one found to give praise?" (See v. 18.)

Lead the group in a time of silent confession for failure to praise God for all the good He brings into our lives. Conclude the silent prayers with a brief summary of this confession: **Forgive us, Lord, for our failure to recognize Your goodness and power in our world. Help us to become more aware of all You do for us.**

Step 2—Praise: An Expression of Faith (10 Minutes)

Introduce this segment by instructing participants to listen for the powerful results of the praise of God's people in an incident during the reign of King Jehoshaphat. Then read aloud (with feeling) the dramatic story of the defense of Jerusalem against the combined armies of Ammon, Moab, and Edom (Seir), as told in 2 Chronicles 20:1-22. After reading the passage, show the top part of the "Praise: An Expression of Faith" transparency, and ask the first question: What was the problem Jehoshaphat faced? (His forces were outnumbered by the attacking armies, and he did not know what to do.)

Continue uncovering questions, one at a time, inviting responses from group members. After all have been answered, share this comment: **We often think of praise as our response *after* God has done something for us. Instead, we need to realize that praising God is our recognition that God is in control, even *before* we have seen the results of His involvement in our circumstances.**

Option: Conversational Praise

This option will add 10 minutes to the Step 2 section.

Ask the group to silently read Psalm 145. Then lead the group in a brief time of praise, praying conversationally. Remind people of the guidelines for conversational prayer shared in Session 4:

- Use only informal, conversational language phrased as personal conversation with our loving heavenly Father.
- Address only one topic or concern in any single prayer, allowing others to interject their thoughts and feelings.
- Before raising a new topic, at least one person should agree in prayer about the issue raised in the previous person's prayer.

Note: If you are completing this session in one meeting, ignore this break and continue with Step 3.

Two-Meeting Track: If you want to spread this session over two meetings, STOP here and close in prayer. Inform group members that your last meeting in this series will focus on how praising God helps us become more aware of His presence and involvement in our lives.

Start Option: Sharing What You've Learned (10 Minutes)

Begin your second meeting by inviting group members to form groups of no more than five people and share with each other one or two ways in which these sessions on prayer have been helpful. If time permits, take two or three minutes to invite volunteers to share with the whole class what they have just told their small group. Then continue with Step 3 and conclude the session.

Step 3—Praise: Stirring Awareness of His Presence (15 Minutes)

Introduce this segment by sharing the situation described in Acts 4:14-23: Miracles were being done through the apostles, but persecution was increasing. Peter and John had been jailed and threatened as a result of the healing of a lame man and their bold preaching about Jesus. After their release, they met with other believers and prayed the prayer which begins in verse 24.

Read aloud Acts 4:24-31. Then ask people to form groups of no more than five people in each group and discuss the following question: **What was the significance of the believers telling God the historical information (vv. 24-28) in this prayer?** Obviously, God was already fully aware of having created everything; He knew the quote from Psalms, as well as the circumstances surrounding Jesus' death. So, why did the believers preface their request (vv. 29,30) with this declaration? Allow several minutes for groups to share ideas, then invite volunteers to report on their conclusions.

While the passage does not state a reason *why* these believers prayed as they did, it is clear that their adoration and praise of God (vv. 24,25), their quoting of Scripture which relates to their current circumstances (vv. 25,26), and their description of a situation in which they had seen evidence of God's sovereignty overcome powerful opposition (vv. 27,28) were expressions of truths *they* needed to hear. Before they could truly believe that God would honor their immediate requests, they needed to be reminded of God's greatness, of relevant insights from God's Word and of God's powerful actions that they had personally experienced in other situations.

Letter on the chalkboard or an overhead transparency: **If we don't praise, we won't believe.** Then ask, **How accurate is that statement?** (Basically, until a person recognizes God's power and His goodness, it is impossible to pray with any expectation of God hearing and responding to a request.)

Then, add to the chalkboard or transparency the implication of this truth: **If you are having a hard time believing, start praising!** Point out that the best way to build faith is to shift our focus from the circumstances of the problem we face and concentrate on the attributes and actions of God.

Conclude this section by reminding participants of the night Jesus' disciples were caught in a storm on the Sea of Galilee. Ask **When Jesus walked out to the disciples' boat, and Peter stepped out onto the surface of the water and began walking to Jesus, what caused Peter to start sinking?** (Matthew 14:30 says, "But when he (Peter) saw the wind, he was afraid....") When Peter took his eyes off Jesus and focused on his circumstances, his faith wavered. But he still had enough trust to recognize Jesus as Lord, and to cry out, "Lord, save me!" Even when our faith is imperfect and doubts arise, God still responds.

Option: Faith Building Praise

This option will add 5 minutes to the Step 3 section.

Lead the group in compiling a list of God's attributes and actions which believers ought to think about instead of focusing attention on circumstances. Divide the chalkboard or an overhead transparency into two columns, "God's Attributes" and "God's Actions" in which to list the items group members suggest. Encourage people to think of specific ways in which God has acted on their behalf.

Step 4 Option—When We Praise (10 Minutes)

Divide the room into three sections, and assign the small groups in each section one of three ways to praise God:

- Reading and meditating on a psalm or other Scripture passage that expresses praise to God;
- Singing worship songs or hymns of praise;
- Praying in our own words to praise God for His attributes and actions.

Instruct group members to share with each other times they have experienced praise in the way they have been assigned to consider. Encourage people to tell what they have discovered to be meaningful about that type of praise.

Conclude this segment by leading the group in one of the three expressions of praise. For example, have everyone join in reading Psalm 136, with a different person reading the first part of each verse, and the full class joining together in reading, "His love endures forever."

Getting Personal

(5 minutes)

Distribute blank paper to each person, along with a pencil or pen for everyone who needs one. Then give these instructions: Take some time now to write a letter of praise to God. Think again of the doxology with which we conclude the Lord's Prayer: "For yours is the kingdom and the power and the glory forever. Amen" (Matthew 6:13). Use the three concepts in that statement to express your praise:

- Kingdom—First, include in your letter statements of praise for God's authority as King, not only of all heaven and earth, but of your life circumstances, as well.
- Power—Second, write about His great power and the ways He has shown that for your benefit.
- Glory—And third, write about reasons you have discovered that God is worthy of our honor and praise.

Allow six or seven minutes for people to write, then invite volunteers to read aloud a sentence from their letters praising God as King. As each sentence is read, lead the group in responding, "His kingdom endures forever!"

Repeat similarly with sentences about God's power, and then His glory, having the group respond, "His power endures forever," and then "His glory endures forever."

Getting Personal Option: Give Thanks

This option will add 5 minutes to the Getting Personal section.

Just as Jesus set an example of giving thanks before He multiplied the loaves and fishes and when He passed around the cup and the bread at His last supper with the disciples, we too should heed Paul's instruction to "Give thanks in all circumstances" (1 Thessalonians 5:18). Lead the group in a closing time of one-sentence prayers of thanks.

Dismiss the session by reading this famous quote from John Bunyan, author of *Pilgrim's Progress*: **"Prayer is a sincere, sensitive, affectionate pouring out of the soul to God, through Christ, in the strength and assistance of the Spirit, for such things as God has promised."**

Praising God Is...

Expressing Approval, Admiration, Honor and Reverence for Him.

A Few Insights About Praise:

<u>Psalm 100</u>   <u>Ephesians 1:3-8</u>

- ....   - ....

- ....   - ....

- ....   - ....

A Few Reasons We Are to Praise God:

"Great is the Lord, and most worthy of praise" (Psalm 48:1).

Psalm 28:6-9

....

....

....

Psalm 34:1-7

....

....

....

Psalm 47

....

....

....

Acts 3:1-10

....

....

....

Revelation 4:8-11

....

....

....

Praise: An Expression of Faith

2 Chronicles 20:1-22

1. What was the problem Jehoshaphat faced? (vv. 10-12)

....

....

....

2. What was the promise God made? (vv. 15-17)

....

....

....

3. What was the response of Jehoshaphat and the people to God's promise?
   vv. 18,19)

....

....

....

4. What instructions did Jehoshaphat give on the day of the battle? (v. 20)

....

....

....

5. What action did the men take who Jehoshaphat had appointed? (v. 21)

....

....

....

6. What was the result? (v. 22)

....

....

....

7. Based on this incident, what course of action should we take when facing problems
   today?

....

....

....

Learn to Fight on Your Knees.

There's a battle raging, an unseen struggle in the heavens that affects the way we live as Christians. But how can you fight against a force that can't be seen, an invisible enemy desperate to foil God's plan? The answer is prayer. Advance the cause of Christ around the world through these factual, biblical guides from Regal Books and Gospel Light.

Regal Books
A Division of Gospel Light

Warfare Prayer
C. Peter Wagner
Book One of the
"Prayer Warrior" Series

A biblical and factual guide to strategic-level spiritual warfare. This book will help you seek God's power and protection in the battle to build His kingdom.
Paperback
ISBN 08307.15134 • $9.99
Video Seminar • SPCN 85116.00612 • $29.99

Prayer Shield
C. Peter Wagner
Book Two of the
"Prayer Warrior" Series

Here is a tool to help you teach lay people to intercede in prayer for you and your ministry.
Paperback
ISBN 08307.15142 • $9.99
Video Seminar
SPCN 85116.00620 • $29.99

Breaking Strongholds in Your City
Edited by C. Peter Wagner
Book Three of the
"Prayer Warrior" Series

Learn how to identify the enemy's territory in your city through "spiritual mapping". Includes practical steps to help you pray against these dark strongholds.
Paperback
ISBN 08307.16386 • $9.99
Video Seminar • SPCN 85116.00647 • $29.99

Churches That Pray
C. Peter Wagner
Book Four of the
"Prayer Warrior" Series

Take a comprehensive look at corporate prayer and see how new forms of prayer can break down the walls between the church and the community—locally and globally.
Paperback
ISBN 08307.16580 • $9.99
Video Seminar
SPCN 85116.00639 • $29.99

Engaging the Enemy
Edited by C. Peter Wagner

John Dawson, Peter Wagner and 16 others provide guidance based on their experiences with territorial spirits.
Paperback
ISBN 08307.17692 • $9.99

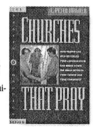

Healing America's Wounds
John Dawson

This is an intercessor's handbook, a guide to taking part in what God is doing today. Learn how healing the wounds of sexual conflict, divisive Christians, political polarization and racial tension through "identification-al repentance" is occurring.
Paperback
ISBN 08307.16939 • $10.99

The Voice of God
Cindy Jacobs

The Voice of God cuts through the confusion about prophecy and provides an uplifting biblical picture of what it means to hear and act upon our Master's voice.
Hardcover
ISBN 08307.17412 • $15.99

Wrestling with Dark Angels
Compiled by C. Peter Wagner and F. Douglas Pennoyer

Spiritual warfare is going on all around you. This collection of essays helps you fight back with a solid understanding of the spiritual realm.
Paperback
ISBN 08307.14464 • $12.99

That None Should Perish
Ed Silvoso

Learn the powerful principles of "Prayer Evangelism" and discover a practical and strategic plan to bring the gospel to your entire community.
Trade
ISBN 08307.16904 • $10.99

My Family's Prayer Calendar
Shirley Dobson and Pat Verbal

This delightful, best-selling calendar gives a new prayer item or activity to share with your child every day. A calendar with quality time built in! Includes more than 60 stickers for special days.
Wall Calendar
SPCN 25116.08448 • $9.99
Merchandiser (pkg. of 10)
25116.09010 • CM/20 $199.80

The Lord's Prayer Coloring Book
Created by Shirley Dobson

The Lord's Prayer Coloring Book is a fun way to teach kids the Lord's Prayer. Features a child's prayer on every page as well as discussion starters for parents or teachers, to help them guide their children.
Coloring Book
SPCN 25116.08987 • .99¢
Merchandiser
(pkg. of 50)
25116.09002
$99.00 CM/100

My Prayer Coloring Book
Created by Shirley Dobson

Now you can turn play time into prayer time. **My Prayer Coloring Book** is a fun way to teach kids that they can pray all through the day.
Coloring Book
SPCN 25116.08251 • .99¢

Giving Meaning to Your Child's Prayer Life

With this booklet, teachers and parents can help children learn how to pray meaningfully and enjoyably.
Paperback
SPCN 25116.05422 • .49¢

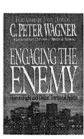

Required Reading for Prayer Warriors

Spreading the Fire
C. Peter Wagner
Book I in the Acts of the Holy Spirit Series.

Take an in-depth, verse-by-verse look at the first eight chapters of Acts, and gain a firm understanding of the Holy Spirit's direction for today's Church. Each chapter directs readers toward a deeper understanding and personal application.
Hardcover • ISBN 08307.17102 • $15.99

Lighting the World
C. Peter Wagner
Book II in the Acts of the Holy Spirit Series.

Book II of Wagner's contemporary look at the central chapters (9-15) of Acts demonstrates the powerful, practical plans that God lays out for Christians, as the gospel spreads out to Samaria.
Hardcover • ISBN 08307.17188 • $15.99

Blazing the Way
C. Peter Wagner
Book III in the Acts of the Holy Spirit Series.

Discover how the first church overcame cultural barriers and Satan's stronghold to bring the Gospel to the world. Examines the final chapters of Acts and shows how they apply today.
Hardcover • ISBN 08307.17196 • $15.99

Resurrecting Hope
John Perkins with Jo Kadlecek

Experience and learn from the inspiring stories of 10 urban ministries that reached out in love to their cities.
Hardcover • ISBN 08307.17757 • $15.99

Your Spiritual Gifts Can Help Your Church Grow
C. Peter Wagner

This new edition of the best-selling classic has been revised and expanded. Includes a spiritual gifts questionnaire to help you discover your own gifts.
Paperback • ISBN 08307.16815 • $10.99

Your Spiritual Gifts Can Help Your Church Grow Group Study Guide
C. Peter Wagner

An easy-to-use study guide that helps you discover your spiritual gifts and how to use them in your church.
Manual • ISBN 08307.17587 • $15.99

Finding Your Spiritual Gifts
The Wagner-Modified Houts Questionnaire
C. Peter Wagner

An easy-to-use questionnaire that guides you in finding and understanding your spiritual gifts.
Questionnaire
ISBN 08307.17:
$3.99
Merchandiser
(pkg. of 50)
T5409 CM150
$199.50

The Names of the Holy Spirit
Elmer L. Towns

Come closer to the Holy Spirit by understanding how his names reflect His ministry throughout God's Word.
Paperback • ISBN 08307.16769 • $9.99
Group Study Guide
ISBN 08307.15843 • $16.99
Video Study Package
SPCN 85116.00701 • $49.99

Living Free in Christ
Neil T. Anderson

Includes study guide and 2 videos

36 Scripture readings and prayers that will transform your thoughts about God, about yourself, about your purpose here on earth.
Paperback • ISBN 08307.16394 • $10.99

Setting Your Church Free
Neil T. Anderson and Charles Mylander

Now pastors and church leaders can apply the powerful principles from *Victory over the Darkness* to lead their churches to freedom.
Hardcover • ISBN 08307.16556 • $16.99

Victory over the Darkness
Neil T. Anderson

Dr. Neil Anderson shows that we have the power to conquer the darkness, once we know who we are in Christ.
Paperback • ISBN 08307.13751 • $9.99
Study Guide • ISBN 08307.16696 • $8.99

Helping Others Find Freedom in Christ
Neil T. Anderson

Learn to share the "the steps to Freedom" with others with this guide.
Hardcover • ISBN 08307.17404 • $16.99

Breaking Through to Spiritual Maturity
Neil T. Anderson

Take possession of the victory Christ freely offers and mature in your faith with this 13-to-24 week course. Based on the best-seller *Victory over the Darkness* and *The Bondage Breaker*.
Manual • ISBN 08307.15312 • $16.99

Concerts of Prayer
David Bryant

Harness the tremendous power of group prayer through your own concert of prayer.
Paperback
ISBN 08307.13018
$9.99

The Heart of Praise
Jack Hayford

You'll become more like Him whom you worship. 60 daily readings based on Psalms with enriching stories.
Paperback
ISBN 08307.16092 • $5.99

The Mary Miracle
Jack Hayford

Every believer, filled with God's spirit and confessing Jesus as savior, can bring healing and hope to a dying world.
Hardcover
ISBN 08307.16521
$12.99

The Kingdom and the Power
Edited by Gary Greig and Kevin Springer

This book takes the debate over "signs and wonders" to a new level of biblical scholarship.
Trade • ISBN 08307.16343 • $19.99

World Missions Map

A great way to remember to pray for God's workers around the world. Includes information about unreached peoples.
ISBN 08307.14987 • $7.99